Who is This Man

Who is This Man

A Journey Through Alzheimer's

Edna Eades, RN

Xlibris Corporation
1-888-795-4274
www.Xlibris.com
Orders@Xlibris.com
46740

Contents

Preface 11

The Pivotal Moment... 13

A Life Before Alzheimer's 21

A Life Within Alzheimer's 83

Epilogue... 155

The Golden Rule Revisited... 161

Medication Guidelines for Caregivers............................. 163

Practical Advice for Caregivers 169

Caregiver Care 173

Dedication

This book is dedicated to Jim Porter (1885-1970). I am forever grateful to Jim. He had no children and took in my father as his own son. Jim fed and clothed him, taught him about life, and taught him how to work. Because of Jim, my father was able to overcome abandonment and hardship. Jim set a positive example and gave young Ray a future. What Jim taught my father was passed on to me, to my children, and will be passed on to future generations. Thank you Jim for taking in a boy and turning him into a man.

I want to acknowledge my editors, Barbara March and Sara Gooch of Deep Creek Editing, www.deepcreekediting.com. Without them this book would still be spread in bits and pieces all over my floor. Thank you for the direction when I didn't know how to proceed and for seeing me through to its completion.

Preface

Tabor's Medical Dictionary describes the inner changes that occur in Alzheimer's: "A chronic, organic mental disorder, a form of pre-senile dementia due to atrophy of the frontal and occipital lobes [that] involves progressive, irreversible loss of memory, deterioration of mental functions, apathy, speech and gait disturbances, and disorientation. Course [of the disease] may take from a few months to four to five years to progress to complete loss of intellectual function."

In a *Time* magazine article, Roger Rosenblatt describes the outward changes: "Such fascinating stages. Initially there is a kind of troubled yet sweet awareness that the clock of the patient's mind is a few seconds off. Then an encroaching recognition of loss of function becomes less recognition and greater loss. Soon words and phrases are looped, like mad lines from a post-modern play; then Tourette's like bursts . . . some comprehensible, some vile; then less of that, less of everything, until the mind is concentrated down to a curious stare."

The changes we saw in my dad were a combination of major shifts in mood and behavior coupled with delusions, clinginess, repetitive questions and actions. We watched as the stages occurred mentally, physically, and emotionally as he lost his sense of direction, his spontaneity, and his ability to think abstractly. Then he lost tangible things like his glasses, car keys, and shoes. Ultimately he lost himself.

This is the story of my family's journey through Alzheimer's. We lived it day-by-day and year-by-year to the end, but your journey may be just beginning. I wrote this book to illustrate things we learned the hard way, to help you distinguish interventions that compound rather than improve Alzheimer's symptoms, and to show you what methods worked and why they worked. My desire is to prove that there is help for the patient and hope for the family. If anything in my dad's story makes a difference in the lives of others, then the hell we lived through was not in vain. By telling my dad's story, I speak for those who cannot speak for themselves.

At the current rate, researchers project that by the year 2050 in the United States, eleven to sixteen million people age sixty-five and older will be Alzheimer's patients. Thankfully, research is ongoing and providing new insight and information for preventing, diagnosing, and treating the disease. This and other research may or may not reach fruition in time to help the millions already afflicted with Alzheimer's but will decrease the numbers of Alzheimer's patients and change their treatment protocols. Until then, all too many of us will be face-to-face with Alzheimer's.

When I was student nurse, a down-and-out woman who frequented the emergency room motioned me over to the corner where she was sitting on the floor and said, "You want to learn? I want to tell you something that I hope you never forget. What do you see when you look at me? Shabby clothes? An old drunk? See beyond the alcohol; look into my eyes and see the person inside." Since then, I look beyond the diagnosis to see the person. Look in the eyes of Alzheimer's victims, and you'll see the individuality of each person, who they were before Alzheimer's, and what they have left that Alzheimer's can't touch.

The Pivotal Moment

Change is the way the future enters our lives.

—Henry Hide

Funny how four little words can change your whole world and alter it so much that nothing is the same from that moment on. For our family that pivotal moment came in the fall of 1994 when I called my mother to ask her what time I should pick her up for a birthday party. "Well, things have changed," she said. "Ray has been extremely agitated and uptight, and he's been pacing the floor all night. I'm ready to commit him; I can't spend another night like that."

I threw some clothes on and hopped in my Explorer to drive the thirty-five miles over Big Valley Mountain to McArthur, a small rural town in northeastern California. The red and gold fall leaves were beautiful along the way, but I barely noticed them. I was too intent on wondering what had happened. Whatever it was must have been major because my mother usually kept problems bottled up inside her. She was fiercely independent and not the type to seek help from anyone. I also knew that it took a lot to make my usually mellow, eighty-four-year-old dad mad.

When I arrived, my frail seventy-eight-year-old mother met me at the door looking exhausted, choking back tears, and sobbing. My dad was pacing the floor, clenching his fist, and chewing his jaw in anger. He was shaking uncontrollably. He shouted, "If I had a gun, I'd kill the SOB!"

"Who? Who would you kill?" I asked.

He stopped abruptly and said, "I can't remember."

My years as an emergency medical technician taught me to handle the situation and let my feelings catch up with me afterward, so I talked calmly to my dad until he settled down. He sat with his elbows propped on his knees and his head, with its thick white hair, hanging down between his oversized hands.

He looked up at me and said, "I'm not a doctor, but I think I am going crazy. There's something wrong with me, and no one has come to help me."

I assured him that I wanted to help him and asked him, "Would you be willing to go to the hospital and see a doctor who is a friend of mine?" To my surprise, he jumped up, and eagerly followed me to the car.

"Finally someone has come to help me! I'm getting crazy in the head, you know," he said.

It was a brief ride to the local hospital two miles away. My mother gave the receptionist Dad's insurance card and filled out the paperwork. When we were taken back to the emergency room, my dad looked the picture of health with his six-foot-two frame and his arms still muscular from years of working as a logger. He had worked hard to maintain his ideal weight of 185 pounds and always bragged that he weighed the same as when he played football in high school. He sat propped up on a gurney, with his long legs and size twelve shoes hanging out over the end. Dad was very cooperative. When the doctor finished examining him, he handed Dad a plastic cup and asked him for a urine specimen.

My dad rolled up his sleeve and said, "Sure, take as much as you want." Previously, we would have thought that he had not heard correctly since he was nearly deaf from running a power saw in the woods for years as a timber faller.

The doctor admitted him for overnight observation and tests. As the emergency medical technicians wheeled my dad down the hall, he smiled, shook their hands and thanked them for the ride.

While my mother spoke with the doctor, I took a moment to let it all sink in. I was still reeling from the day's events. I couldn't help but think how different it was to be the family of the patient. I was used to being the nurse. This time it was different. This was not just another routine admission. This was my dad. Not just my dad, but a real father. I didn't have one bad memory of him. I respected, loved, and admired him. He was the one who had always looked out for my best interests. I was not ready for the role reversal.

The nurse said to me, "You look more like you need admission than your dad does." It was no wonder. I knew that Alzheimer's was not just simply "Old Timers" as some people refer to it. It was more than forgetfulness in old age. Our family was familiar with the damage Alzheimer's leaves. No longer could we think that the Alzheimer's that had touched almost all of my dad's entire family had bypassed him. We knew that like an unwelcome, invisible, intruder, Alzheimer's steps in uninvited and stays way too long. Not only that, Alzheimer's takes more and more of who a person is, until there is nothing left to take. We knew our lives would never be the same again.

As mother and I walked out of the hospital, we could only focus on one question, "What lies ahead?" I was reminded of a pharmaceutical ad that showed a monstrous red giant on the horizon with two frightened people standing in front of it with the caption, "Oh no! Here come circumstances beyond our control!" Our nightmare of being powerless to control what was happening to us had begun. Alzheimer's had stuck its foot in the door leaving us to pick up the shattered remains of our lives.

After I left my mother off at home, my thoughts turned to a quotation I'd read in USA Weekend regarding Alzheimer's: "Americans fear Alzheimer's more than death, a diagnosis of cancer, job loss, or stock market crash." I was no different. Medical essayist Dr. Lewis Thomas called Alzheimer's the "disease of the century."

My mother and I came face to face with the fact that my dad had Alzheimer's after all the tests were completed, and all the other causes explaining his behavior were ruled out. He had no infection or diagnosis that would alter his mental state. My dad had always been healthy and unaffected by whatever came at him. He had always been strong and able to defend himself. But up to this point in his life, whatever he faced was tangible. He had no defense against Alzheimer's because it was not an outward intruder but attacked from within. We could no longer deny our suspicions or refuse to accept his diagnosis. We could no longer attribute his off-the-wall answers to his hearing problems.

Knowing and accepting that my dad had Alzheimer's made me totally at odds with myself. As a nurse, I understood. As a daughter, I was still in denial. This was not a problem I could leave at work and go home and forget. This was not an acute illness that was going to get better and go away. It was there and it was inescapable. It was chronic and irreversible.

Alzheimer's. Just a word, right? Not to me. I wish that Alzheimer's had been just another medical term, just more terminology. It wasn't that easy. I was altogether too familiar with Alzheimer's because of our family history. With it came connotations of loss of abilities, loss of self-control, and deterioration.

My memories of my Grandma Sally, my paternal grandmother, are of her either in bed or in a wheelchair. She was always more like a great-great-grandmother than a grandmother. She was a month short of 104 when she died. Even as a child, I only saw her in a rest home. I can still smell the stale urine as she lay bedridden during the last forty years of her life. She was at her best at family dinners, when my dad and his brothers brought her in a wheelchair to my aunt and uncle's home for Mother's Day. She sat at the table toothlessly gumming whatever was on her plate until it was time for my uncles to load her in the car and take her back to the rest home. Communication with her was pretty much one sided. Occasionally she would laugh if my mother teased her, but she never initiated conversation. She couldn't remember what happened a few minutes before and had no idea what year it was but could recall in detail the dress she wore to Sunday school as a small child.

There was a century between us and a distance that couldn't be bridged. She looked at me, and I looked at her. I had no idea what she was thinking, and she barely knew who I was. She was just there, that was all. After dinner was over and we were on our way home, my dad always shook his head and made the same statement. "I never want to live like that. I never want to be a burden to anyone." Then he would snap his fingers for emphasis as he said, "When my time is up, I want to go just like that."

I remember my parents coming home from a visit to one of my dad's brothers and telling us how they were awakened in the middle of the night by my aunt shouting, "No. Stop! Don't pee in there. That's not the bathroom; that's the closet." That was only the beginning of my dad seeing his family, like dominoes, fall one after another, to the power of Alzheimer's.

I went to visit my Uncle Reuel in a rest home and listened as the nurse bragged to me that they had finally found the right combination of medications for him. My parents told me that he had been violent when not chemically or physically restrained. I barely recognized him, an expressionless zombie, zonked on medications, staring into space like something out of the movie, "Awakenings." I barely recognized the uncle who used to come to our house to work on projects with my dad. He was no longer my uncle who loved to tell jokes. He wasn't violent, but his condition wasn't anything to brag about. My dad grieved at the changes he saw in him.

My dad's youngest brother Romaine had started chain smoking at the age of fourteen. He was taller than my dad, but eventually he was bent in half in his old age. Even though he still lived at home, he had cigarette burns on his rumbled polyester pants, food stuck on his face, and drool running down his plaid shirt. He didn't recognize me, his niece whom he had seen frequently all his life. He died of congestive heart failure in his eighties, with a carton of cigarettes unopened on his nightstand because he'd forgotten he smoked.

My dad's last living sibling, Rondel, was confined to a bed in a rest home with Parkinson's and Alzheimer's, unable to communicate except to squeeze someone's hand. One of Dad's sisters, Electa, worked in a hospital many years, devoting her life to caring for others. After that she cared for the elderly in her own home. Later, she was unable even to care for herself.

My father's oldest sister Cametrice, an artist who painted delicate ceramic figurines, died of organic brain syndrome. Knowing my family's history, I would rather die in an auto accident than to live to my eighties and become a victim of Alzheimer's.

Until now my dad was the only one who had escaped that family history. He seemed somehow immune. We had been so thankful that even though Alzheimer's had stolen his brothers and sisters, he remained unscathed. But now we were face to face with Alzheimer's disease. I realized that what had been normal in my grandmother, and even acceptable in my aunts and uncles, was suddenly unfathomable in my dad.

I thought of all the patients I had seen and cared for over the years as a nurse's aide and later as a nurse. One lady always sat by the door of the long-term facility where I did my student nursing time. She cursed constantly. Filthy words poured from her mouth. When anyone walked by, all they heard was her profanity because any other form of communication was gone. Other residents were non-communicative and stared into space with no recognition of anyone or anything. Present in body but not in mind. One lady in "memory care" crawled on the floor like a baby; others wore diapers. Most had to be fed like birds, responding only to open their mouths. One woman never stopped crying. Others only followed you with their eyes, maybe in an attempt to see if they could trust you. They were ready to defend themselves by scratching or biting if they thought someone threatened to hurt them. Others were vegetables curled up in the fetal position, shells of their former selves, waiting to die. I had seen too much. I didn't want my dad to fit in any of those categories. I tried to put those memories out of my mind, but I couldn't. They haunted me.

I lay awake, unable to sleep, thinking of the enormity of it all. My thoughts raced through the worst-case scenarios. The longer I dwelt on Alzheimer's, the bigger it became. The first night, my mind was in high gear, like an automobile with a manual transmission stuck in a gear you can't shift down. Like being trapped in a maze with no way out, there were no answers. The future became bleaker as I lay awake in those wee hours of the morning. I realized that like my niece, who panicked when she heard there was a dangerous escapee on the loose from a prison near the Oregon border, I was making it bigger than it was. That niece bolted and barricaded the doors of her house because she lived on the highway near the California and Oregon border. She knew the prisoner would be arriving any minute, so she stood in the dark with a loaded gun ready to defend herself and her two small children who were clinging to her side. The escaped convict became her only focus. The next morning she heard that the escape had taken place on the Washington border and nowhere near her house. She lost a night of sleep for nothing because of her fear. An escaped convict "on the Oregon border" became bigger than life to her as she focused only on what might happen.

The first night I cried all night. The second night, I lay awake thinking of the unfairness and hopelessness of Alzheimer's. I worried about the future, what it held for my dad and what it held for us. I lay awake for three nights dwelling on Alzheimer's. After those first horrible nights, I researched everything I could about Alzheimer's in books and on the Internet.

Whatever I knew about Alzheimer's before was intensified by my research on the subject. As I tried to sleep, the information I found kept running through my thoughts. It all came down to this. The key message in Alzheimer's research is that there is no cure and very little hope. The patient will deteriorate instead of improve. Alzheimer's is progressive. Caregivers wear out from emotional and physical exhaustion. Patients deteriorate mentally while remaining physically healthy for years. No cure. Little hope. Like neon lights, these frightening thoughts flashed before my eyes and were branded on my mind.

The more research I did, the more depressed I became. Fear immobilized me. It made me feel that Alzheimer's was bigger than anyone's ability to deal with it. At times I couldn't even see the computer screen for the tears rolling down my cheeks. I pictured my dad as a vegetable curled up in a fetal position. The emotions were overpowering. I felt like a friend who, when I asked how she was, said, "I'm having my own personal tsunami."

The more I focused on it, the bleaker the future seemed. Alzheimer's got bigger. The nights were as long as my endless questions, "Why God?" and "How can this be happening to us?"

Sometime before dawn on the fourth night, I discovered I was only focusing on the worst-case scenarios. I recognized it was a matter of perspective, and my perspective was all out of focus. The world had not fallen off its axis. I realized that the real question was not "How big is Alzheimer's?" but "How big is God?"

I remembered an instance at a medical center where I worked. The reception area had to be modified for patient confidentiality because phone calls for referrals could be heard in the waiting room. The reception area had a half-moon shaped counter and needed to be enclosed with rounded glass above the counter. The maintenance man was called in to fix it. After looking at the size and complexity of the job he said, "This job is too big for me. This is beyond my area of expertise. You'll have to call someone else."

The administrator called in a contractor. He took one look at it and said, "Oh, it's nothing. A piece of cake. How soon do you want me to start?" He got right to work and completed it without a problem. This example helped me come to the conclusion that what was overwhelming to me was no problem to God.

I looked back over the years to the various impossible situations in which we had done all we could do and had no answers. Like other families, none of us were immune to problems. Sometimes we were just cruising along like a bird, minding our own business, and then wham, we flew into a window, knocked to the ground by the unexpected. Sometimes just a phone call brought news that caught us off guard. It seemed at times that our problems were like mountain ranges; we would get over one and another would loom up ahead. And always we wanted a way out rather than to have to go through the pain and the process. It was like wanting our teeth filled without having to have an injection or a dentist's drill. We had tight spots where we were in a bind with no solutions, where we were suddenly helpless to control what was happening to us. We wanted an easy out, but instead we found ourselves with a Mount Everest to climb—a mountain that seemed insurmountable, immovable, impossible, with no way out and no way around.

When we tried to change a bad situation on our own and realized there was absolutely no way out, God always made a way through. My kids had a name for these circumstances. They called them "Red Sea situations" after the story of the Israelites who were trapped at the Red Sea, surrounded by water in front of them, mountains on the side, and the Egyptians in hot pursuit. They were trapped, in a bind, with no escape, and the outcome looked pretty grim. We know what happened, that God opened the Red Sea and they walked across on dry land and saw their enemies defeated. "God made a way in the sea, and a path in the mighty waters," (Jeremiah 43:16). Consequently when we were trapped in an impossible situation, our two choices were to focus on the fear, or focus on faith that God would somehow get us through.

Slowly, I began to get things into perspective. I realized I had forgotten this quote, "This is a slight thing in the eyes of the Lord," (II Kings 3:18). Like the reception area, I left my problems in the hands of the expert. When I looked up instead of focusing down, when I took my eyes off the immensity of the circumstances, the turmoil was gone. I came to grips with the fact that what is beyond our area of expertise—too big for us to fix—is not beyond God's ability.

No matter how big and formidable Alzheimer's is, no matter how grim the situation, and how helpless we think we are, it is not bigger than God's ability to handle it. He had never let us down before; why should this be any different? So on the fourth night, in the early hours of the morning, I wiped away my tears and acknowledged that God was bigger than Alzheimer's.

It was the end of sleeplessness and the beginning of trust. I decided to take God at his word and "be not anxious about any person, place or thing,"(Philippians 4:6). I came to the conclusion that no matter how scary Alzheimer's was, God hadn't deserted us and left us to fend for ourselves. No matter how foreboding and devastating Alzheimer's was, I knew from past experience that I could trust God. I remembered this phrase, "What times I am afraid, I will trust in thee," (Psalms 56:3). I came to grips with the fact that God was bigger than my fears. I slept trusting my dad to the same God that protected my daughter from injury on the freeway when she skidded on ice on a four-lane freeway and crossed over into oncoming lanes of traffic. I knew that whatever we faced, God would supply our needs and give us the resources, wisdom, and strength to get us through. We had seen amazing answers from God in the past, why should this be any different? I knew that God was bigger than any situation we would face in the future. I accepted that God is bigger than the question, "What lies ahead?"

A Life Before Alzheimer's

The richest man, whatever his lot, is the one who's content with what he has got.

—Dutch saying

Ray Granville Methvin was born to Sally and Dorr Methvin on March 6, 1910. He was their fifth child. They already had two daughters, Cametrice and Electa, and two sons, Reuel, and Rondel, all approximately two years apart.

Ray was born in a farmhouse on a ranch in the high desert frontier of Modoc County, near Alturas, California. He was delivered by his paternal grandmother in the middle of the night, a huge baby with big hands and feet. She estimated his weight at sixteen pounds. Before signing the birth certificate, she checked the required boxes, including one labeled "legitimate."

The previous baby, Rondel, had been two months premature. He was so small that his grandmother wrapped him in cotton batting and put him in a drawer near the wood stove to keep him warm. Ray was a giant by comparison.

Ray's mother Sally said that she didn't mind having a baby as big as Ray, but she had a cold, and it was hard to breath during the delivery. She named him Ray Granville Methvin, but he would only learn his true middle name years later when he needed a copy of his birth certificate to join the army. Sally forgot his middle name was Granville and always told him his middle name was Hubard.

Sally was six years older than her husband Dorr, who was thirty-two. When she was fifteen, she wanted to become a nun, and she joined a Catholic convent in Eugene, Oregon. Her plans changed when she met Dorr. The family history is vague on the circumstances of their meeting. They knew each other for only three or four months before marrying. They were married at her parents' home in a small wedding with only a few close friends and relatives. The announcement in the *Alturas Plaindealer* read "Happy Wedding" and announced that the nuptial knot had been tied on November 9, 1902.

Sally's father, Colonel William Thompson, was described in a letter to the editor of the *Modoc Record* years later as "pioneer, gunfighter, Indian fighter." Little is known about Sally's mother, Libby. She blended into the background like most women of her time. In Colonel William Thomson's book, *Reminiscences of a Pioneer*, he mentions Libby only once in stating that he had married. She died a couple of years after Sally returned to Alturas.

Sally led a sheltered life before she met Dorr. She grew up in a fort in Oregon while her father fought for eight years in the Bannock and Modoc Indian wars. Her family raised race horses, and she told of watching the cowboys as they cared for the horses. She was not required to do much work, so she passed her time playing with kittens, ducks and chickens, and the children of the Indians who worked at the fort.

Two years after my father's birth, his brother Romaine was born. The last child, Dorothy, was born in 1915. She died approximately two years later in the diphtheria epidemic. It must have seemed like history repeating itself, because Sally was the only surviving child when her brothers and sisters died from diphtheria.

Dorr's brother reportedly caused trouble between Sally and Dorr by labeling Sally as lazy. Dorr fell in ill favor with his father-in-law, Colonel Thompson. No one knows what that problem was, but since Sally's father already had two notches in his belt for gunfights, Dorr didn't want to take any chances, so he moved his family near his own parents in Nevada and then on to Boise, Idaho.

One of my dad's earliest memories was when Dorr used a block and tackle to pull their Model T and trailer, loaded with all their possessions, over mountain passes. Dad told of helping drive a steel peg to anchor the ropes. All the children helped, but the family eventually had to ask for assistance from strangers.

The family lived in Boise in a big barn-like house until Sally left with six-year-old Ray and four-year-old Romaine to return to Alturas to her parents. As they were pulling out from the train station, my dad waved to the soldiers on the World War I troop trains. He couldn't have known he was also symbolically waving goodbye to his father and that he would not see his father again for twenty-three years. He would be the only one of the seven siblings to ever see his father again. Dorr left Boise a few days later. Dorr headed east, Sally headed west. At that point, the "nuptial knot" that was already frayed suddenly unraveled. Dorr started a new life without his family.

Before he left Idaho, Dorr farmed out the four oldest children, leaving them wherever he could along the way. Ray's sisters, Cametrice and Electa, were left with families in Boise. His brothers, Reuel, and Rondel, were abandoned in Boise to make it on their own. Cametrice was thirteen, Electa eleven; Reuel was nine, and Rondel was only eight-years-old. Rondel lived with a man who was cruel to him, and Reuel survived on the street. Both had to steal corn and jam and other food to live. They worked for a dairy for a while but did not get paid. Colonel Thompson came by train and took the girls back to Alturas. When Reuel and Rondel were older, their grandfather sent money for them to return to Alturas too.

My father and his younger brother Romaine lived with their mother on their grandparent's homestead near Alturas until their mother remarried and moved to nearby Cedarville.

After Dorr left Idaho, he earned a living as a barber until he established a congregation that could support him as a minister. Approximately three years later, he married Sadie, a woman twenty-two years younger than he and had seven more children. In the process, he changed his name from Methvin to Melvin. His whereabouts remained unknown to his first family until 1938 when he wrote to Cametrice to tell her he had pastored seventeen churches and led many revivals.

Sally was remarried in 1920 to Henry Koch, a Spanish American War Veteran, who managed the Cedarville Hotel. When she moved with him to nearby Cedarville, she did not take her children with her. They were farmed out to other homes. My dad was essentially an orphan before he started school. Sally was happy with her new husband, but he died a couple of years after they were married. He was working as a cook at the hotel and died of ptomaine poisoning. Sally moved back to her father's homestead near Alturas, cleaning houses to earn a living. She later moved to a house he owned in Alturas.

My dad was taken in by the Porter family at the age of six. He became a chore boy for them. They lived on Parker Creek outside of Alturas. At first young Ray lived with Jim Porter's mother Phere, who was elderly and lived alone in a cabin on a creek where she said she was "proving up on a claim." The Porter family wanted someone to live with her because she lived well over a mile away from them. Ray was available day and night to run for help if she needed anything. My dad learned how to relate to others by living as part of the Porter family. When he was seven years old, he lived with Jim Porter's sister, Nettie Pepperdine. One day, Nettie was churning cream and caught her long braid in the cream separator. My dad grabbed an axe and cut off her braid to free her.

Jim Porter took young Ray in and raised him as his own son. Jim was a very kind man. He taught my dad values and how to work on the farm and showed him by example about life. Ray was kept busy with daily chores, caring for the animals, and helping in the kitchen.

My dad remembered quite a bit from his early years with the Porters. He rode one of Jim's horses to grammar school. There was the time when he was nine years old, heading for school, he saw a coyote attacking a calf. He galloped the horse and scared the coyote away, and the calf followed him to school. At the end of the school day, the calf followed him home.

Another time he went ice-skating alone. He fell through the ice, and there was no one there to help him out. He knew he had to come back up where he fell through or he would be trapped under the ice. He got out by swimming back up to the hole he fell through. He managed to scramble out of the water onto the ice and make his way to shore. He walked two miles home in frozen clothes.

Ray lived with Jim Porter until he was nine or ten, then he lived with his mother during the school year, and probably attended Gleason Creek school. He spent his summers on the farm with Jim.

When Ray was eleven years old, he learned to make arrowheads from a local man named Charlie, who explained that the only two tools he needed were "a deer antler and a heavy square of leather." Charlie showed him how to hold the chunk of black glass-like obsidian in his left hand on top of the leather and then put pressure on the obsidian to delicately chip it in the shape of an arrowhead. This new skill intrigued my dad, and he practiced until he could do it flawlessly. It was the beginning of a lifetime hobby.

When he was in the ninth grade Ray worked two hours after school and ten hours on Saturdays relieving the women in a box factory in Alturas. He gave part of his earnings to his mother and used the rest for school supplies. My dad was teased for his ragged clothes and because of that was always quick to defend himself. His older brothers paid for his high school football uniform and graduation suit.

In the summer, my dad learned to do a man's work making huge stacks of loose hay. He estimated the size of the piece of ground for the stack and pitched the hay accordingly as it was brought in from the field by the horses pulling buck rakes. As a haystack grew, he'd stand on top of the stack, calling out, "More hay. More hay." The men used nets and cables pulled by manpower and horses to get the hay to the top of the stack, and an average stack took the crew four to five days to build. They stacked the hay about twenty feet high by sixty feet long and fourteen feet wide. My dad was paid one dollar plus room and board for a twelve-hour day stacking hay.

At Modoc High School, Ray went out for sports and was a very good athlete. In football, his position was right tackle, and he was known as the "Iron Man" for playing every minute of every football game.

His track coach told him that if he would take three steps between hurdles instead of five, he would win. Ray followed the coach's advice, and it worked just like the coach said. At one track meet, Ray set the record in pole-vaulting, but when he ran and made the first jump and landed in the sand pit, his pants split from end to end, exposing more than he wanted the crowd to see. His coach told him that if he left to change he would be disqualified, so he finished the competition and set the record at twelve feet, six inches, which stood for eleven years, until bamboo poles were replaced with fiberglass.

After graduation from Modoc High in 1929, my dad was deputized to transport prisoners from Alturas to San Quentin. He refused to transport female prisoners. He did not want to be alone with the women. "I never wanted to be in that position where they could falsely accuse me of anything." He had seen others accused of rape.

As his grandfather Colonel Thompson got older, he hated the cold winters in Alturas. After Ray graduated from high school, he drove his granddad to Los Angeles for the winters and stayed there with him. During the two-day trip, the colonel would complain that my dad was driving too fast because the Starr car they owned was capable of reaching speeds up to sixty miles an hour. In Los Angeles they rented a guesthouse in the yard of a large family named Dearr. The Dearrs liked to give ice cream parties and serve root beer floats. One of the Dearr daughters invited a seventeen-year-old friend named Ruth to an ice cream party. My dad was twenty-three when he first met his future wife.

When the colonel and Ray returned to Los Angeles for the second winter, my dad decided to attend Curtis Wright Aeronautics School. He worked on transit aircraft to pay half of his tuition. He worked most Saturdays and Sundays with only a few days off. But he still found time to date Ruth. That took a little persistence. She wrote in her diary during that time, "Ray has gone back for the summer, and that's ok by me."

Ray's father deserted him. His mother lived a fairly sheltered life as a child and was ill equipped to handle raising children alone. She was emotionally absent and then remarried and did not take the children with her. His brothers were bitter about being deserted by their father and carried that bitterness to their death. They never recovered from the fact that their father left them to fend for themselves. In spite of all that happened to them though, they were survivors and stuck together. The brothers and sisters left in Idaho made it back to Alturas and were close to their siblings even though they did not grow up together.

Ray overcame his circumstances. He had a positive outlook on life. He worked hard instead of letting resentment and bitterness keep him bound to the past. He looked forward and saved for the future. Because he had no home of his own, he knew the value of saving for one. He knew the value of a college education because he didn't have one. He put in many hours working and putting away money so his children and grandchildren wouldn't have to work as hard as he did to earn a living.

Whatever bad things happened to Ray made him stronger and more able to cope with the next problem that came along. My dad remained unscarred in spite of the hardships. He grew up with no father, yet he was an excellent father to me.

In a recommendation letter written in 1941, John C. Sharp, Sheriff of Modoc County said, "I have known Ray for over twenty years, and in all this time he has been an excellent boy and man, and he has never been in any trouble with the law or otherwise."

Also in 1941, Modoc County Judge A. K. Wylie wrote, "I have been acquainted with Mr. Ray Methvin for many years and have known him since he was a child. He is bright, sober, upright, and trustworthy; absolutely honest in his dealing, and can be relied upon in any work he may undertake; and any consideration or courtesy extended to him in employment will be much appreciated by me. I am confident that he may prove worthy in every respect."

Dad reappeared in Burbank each winter when he drove his grandfather to the warmer climate of southern California. They returned to the cottage they rented from the Dearrs. At the first chance he had, Dad would call on my mother. She was still in high school and not ready for a serious relationship. Dad was persistent. My mother's diary reflected, "I told my mother to tell Ray I wasn't home, but she wouldn't do it." They double dated with her sister, Helen, and Helen's future husband, Chet, and spent time on the beach.

During that time, Dad graduated from Curtis Wright Aeronautics School. In the spring, after he drove his grandfather home to Alturas, my dad returned to his job in the woods for the Red River Lumber Company. After the death of his grandfather, he spent a winter in Seattle working for Kenner Aircraft until the Depression hit and his job was eliminated.

In December 1941, Pearl Harbor was bombed, and our country was at war. Dad drove from Alturas to Klamath Falls, Oregon, to enlist to help defend his country. He joined the Army Air Corp on January 3, 1942. He was stationed in Wichita Falls, Texas, for boot camp. Then he was sent to Fort Lewis, Washington, where he was a private first class and did duty as a guard. Later in 1942, he was transferred to Columbia, South Carolina, as a master mechanic on a trial basis. There he pre-flighted planes and did emergency repairs.

Once, while he was stationed in the South, Ray walked eight miles with a group of soldiers to swim at a college pool. The men were told that if they were late getting back from furlough they would be considered AWOL. Dad was on a bus returning to base when the driver refused to stop for a black man in uniform. Dad told the driver, "Stop this bus right now or you will have me to fight." The driver knew he meant it and stopped to pick up the soldier.

While Dad was stationed in the South, his sister Cametrice, who was living in Alturas, shared the news that she'd received a letter from Winchester, Virginia, from their father. Dad decided to go visit him. When he arrived in the neighborhood and asked directions to his father's house, the person he asked said, "I know who you are because you look just like Dorr."

His half-sister Lillian was fourteen years old at the time. She saw a taxi pull up at the end of their lane and drive off, so she ran out to see who it was. She saw a soldier in uniform walking down the lane. She knew her father had a family by his first marriage because she had overheard her parents talking about it. She instantly knew the soldier must be one of Dorr's sons because there was such a strong resemblance to her father. And as she later remembered, "We were poorer than church mice. It was so cold in the house that we all slept around the wood stove." She awoke every morning to hear her father praying. She heard him ask forgiveness for his treatment of his first family.

Lillian recalled Ray's arrival: "The twins were playing outside. The soldier bent down to me and said, 'You don't know me. I am looking for Dorr Methvin.'" That day was the beginning of a bond between Lillian and Dad that lasted a lifetime. He became closer to her than he was to his own sisters, Electa and Cametrice.

As Ray and Lillian walked back to the house, the twins, who were five years old at the time, came running. Lillian's ten-year-old brother stood back and watched. "Ray picked us up one at a time and set us on a ledge where he could look at us and told us he would love to buy us candy." When the three older siblings arrived, he hugged them and told them he loved them all.

Ray's dad came around the house and father and son shook hands. Dorr told Ray that he was glad to see him. When Ray was introduced to Sadie, Dorr's wife, he immediately liked her. While they waited for her older sister to come home, Lillian ran into the house and put on her only pretty dress before they took pictures.

An amazing thing about my dad was that he wasn't jealous, he loved his half-brothers and sisters and Sadie. Instead of dwelling on what had happened in the past, he had a way being content in the present. That was the last time Ray ever saw his dad, but he visited Sadie years later on a trip to the East Coast after he retired.

Around the time of Ray's visit with his father, my mother's mother died during cancer surgery. My mother's sister Helen had married Chet, and they had their own home. My mother was left alone before she graduated from high school. Her father had been killed in a motorcycle accident when she was six years old. Because teenage Ruth had no way to make the house payments, the house was repossessed.

Parentless, she worked as a cook for room and board and graduated from high school. She worked several jobs and put herself through college, too, and received a degree as a home economics teacher. After graduating from college in Santa Barbara, she decided to move to Beverly, Massachusetts, where her aunt and uncle lived. She chose to ride the Greyhound bus from Burbank to Beverly, partly because of the cost of flying and partly to see the scenery. She started teaching school in Beverly while she lived with her aunt and uncle on their farm.

One day a letter was forwarded to her from Burbank. It was from Ray Methvin. My mother was happy to hear from him and wrote back. In their letters to one another they recalled special times they had had together in Burbank. Dad went to Beverly to visit her on furlough. When he returned to Jacksonville Army Air Field, he wrote to my mother and continued to write while they were apart.

Mother saved all the letters she received from Dad during World War II. These letters give us a glimpse of his time as a soldier and allow us to see his personality, attitudes, and reactions to life during the war years, 1942-1945.

Feb 19, 1943

My Dearest Sweetheart,

Was glad to receive your letter. In fact it was what I needed to cheer me up. It was a grand letter because it had my feet walking on thin air. I thought I was in love before, but so help me God, I never had the warm feeling that I now possess. In fact, I would say, that the symptoms you have given me are almost too much for me to stand. In fact, at this time, I think that I am going to explode with happiness. Think of it, I am afraid to even take a breath, for fear that I might end up in destruction.

Thinking back, I for one never dreamed that I would receive a letter like that from you. It was a grand letter. Before I only received friendly ones and now at last I am receiving the kind of letters that one would dream about. In fact it was my first grand letter from you and I am more than happy that at last you feel for me as I have always felt for you. To me, it is more like a dream, especially after all these years that we have made up our minds and discovered that we wanted each other. As the boys say around here, "Oh! My head." Here's one that feels as though he were intoxicated with happiness.

Today I recognized your letter long before it was called and handed to me. In fact I had to fight myself from reaching out and taking the letter out of the hand of the man calling the mail. Rather strange, isn't it, the way that I recognize your letters?

I guess that you will think that I am lucky. No doubt you will chuckle with that little laugh of yours at what I am about to tell you. There was only one case of mumps in the camp and it had to be in the barracks that I am in. Now there are two cases of measles and they both took place in my barracks. The first day I worked, one came down with the measles and the next day the barracks was again under quarantine and another broke out with the small red spots on his skin and went to the hospital. God only knows who will be the next one; for all I know I may be the lucky one. This time everyone is restricted to the barracks. This being restricted to the barracks is about to get me down, owing to the fact that all I have to do is eat, sleep and get bed sores. In a way, I look for them to lift the restriction on a few of us. At least I hope so, for I am tired of doing bunk fatigue. I have done it for three days and if I have to do much more of this kind of work it will probably end up getting me down.

I am rather pleased to know that I have your Aunt Mina's approval for your hand. I realize that I am a soldier and have to go and do whatever the government tells me to do. I may be here for the duration and then again I may be transferred to the bomb group and go across. You know that I said that it was up to you to decide what you wanted to do. If you want to go ahead and get married, I am only too willing. To be honest with you, I still would rather you stay up there and work than to come down here and live under these cheap conditions. I realize that I may be sent out most any time and this happens to be no place for a woman with ninety thousand love hungry soldiers running up and down the streets. In fact, I know that you will never like the South. I know that I can trust you anywhere, but even though we may have to live apart I would know that you would have someone to look after you up there. But again, I will leave that up to you to decide.

Well I guess that I had better bring this letter to a close or I will not get it in the mail. Give all my love and, if you wish, keep most of it for yourself. Just remember that I love you and that whatever makes you happy is what I want.

You asked me if I ever heard whether Mother received the money. To be honest, I hate to admit it but I am unable to answer your question. I sent her some money for her birthday and Mother's Day and to this day I do not know whether she received it. I have only one letter and a Christmas present from her. I know from experience that she is a poor hand to write or answer letters. I just try to understand and when I write her I never mention it.

Your loving sweetheart, Ray M.

Feb 21, 1943 Columbia Air Force Base

My Dearest Sweetheart,

All that it takes is a letter from you to cheer me up. I always hope that I will be able to hold your love, for it means more to me than anything that I have ever got or ever hope to have. I would like to have you here in my arms, so that I could be in heaven. Still I say that the ten days I spent with you were the happiest days of my life. Now that I know you are going to be mine is enough to make life brighter and more worth living than any time in the past.

I have got more to look forward to, you coming to see me in May and also knowing that you are going to wear my ring with the best of intentions is enough to make me shout out loud as though I were drunk. Even though it is out of the question for me to be with you, I am elated over the fact that I hold your love, respect, admiration, and trust. Is it any wonder that I am better satisfied when I know all these things? Before I had nothing to look forward to but the hum-drum of Army life, and now I have got a lot of happiness coming up and that will be the day you set foot in Columbia. There is also a "rumor" going around that Major Jarvis made the statement that he is going to lose a lot more of his key men within the next month. During the past week we have received three men into the Flight Section who were not able to pass their overseas physical. That means eventually that the ones that are physically fit will have to go regardless of whether they wish to or not. The rumor is proving to be the true from what I saw take place. A large number of the key men of the 96th were transferred into the Bomb Squadron this weekend and have gone to join their squadrons who are slated for overseas duty. In time I may have to go. This war cannot end too fast to suit me.

If and when the time comes for me to go, I just as well take it and like it. Once life was rather monotonous and I longed to go. Now it has changed and I would like to stay, so that

I could be close to you. As you know that I am no better than the next one and the war is as much my war as it is any good American citizen's. If and when that time comes that I do go across I am going to be worthy of my name.

The quarantine will be up a week from this Monday. Regardless of the shortage of help the Dr. said that there would be no work for any of us, owing to the fact that he couldn't take the chance of jeopardizing the whole base. This place is like a prison and the sooner I get back to work the better I will like it. As soon as my restriction is up I am going to see what I can do about the rings. Regardless of whether I go across I want you to have the rings whether I get to place it on your finger or not. If I have to go I want you to have the rings to remember me by.

I read in the paper where you were having cold weather. In fact the paper stated that it was even colder than the figures you gave me. Remember when we forgot about the cold in Beverly when we were together? We had the coldest wave down here in the past week that we have had all winter. It even froze two inches of ice which is exceptionally cold for this section. It has now moderated and is rather warm.

You will never know how close I came to taking my overseas physical. I received a phone call down at Base Operations and was asked if I could pass an overseas examination. I told them that I could and they told me to stand by for another call. We lost five out of the flight section but that call never came for me to go. To be honest with you I feel that I will see foreign soil in six months. I consider it best that I tell you this information so that you can judge accordingly. It is the only fair thing to do but honey do not let it worry you too much. After all, it is my duty to go wherever the government decides to take me without crying about it.

Well, Dear, it is about dinner time and I am running out of words to express my love for you. There shouldn't be any doubt after receiving this letter and if there should be I will undertake another one to vindicate myself.

Now I guess that I had better go to bed so I can dream of you sweetheart. Isn't it going to be grand when we can be together and never have to part?

Give my love to all and if you wish, keep most of it for yourself.

Your Loving Sweetheart, Ray M.

May 28, 1943
A.P.O. 4524 c/o Postmaster

Dearest Sweetheart,

Darling, I am still disappointed over what happened. I am more disappointed that I was transferred at the time you were coming down. I never left Columbia until last night. As for June and our plans for the garden marriage, I doubt that will ever come true. To be honest with you, I doubt if I will be here longer than two months. The only way now that we will ever be united is for you to come to me after school is out. I will try to get a furlough at that time providing it is possible. In fact, I am not able to state facts because I do not know. All I know is that this is a new field without accommodations. In fact, I am tenting tonight.

There is a new rumor going around that we are only going to be here three weeks. I know that we will not go across at that time but probably go to another air base. In fact, I doubt that there is any truth to the rumors. When I first went to Columbia I was only supposed to stay six weeks and I lacked four days of a year of staying.

Whatever is to come, Darling, I have got to make the best of it. After all, I am a soldier and no longer have any rights to say what I would like to do. Just remember that I love you and will keep on loving you regardless of where I am. I may be a soldier but my heart is always with you.

I was in hopes that I would have the opportunity to see you once more. But as you can see that is out of the question. Here I am not allowed any visitors and am restricted to the area.

From now on all my letters will be censored by the Squadron Commander and then re-censored at the A.P.O. No doubt my letters will not sound the way they did in the past. In fact I can not even tell you anything about the trip. All I can say is that I arrived O.K.

Just how long I am going to be here remains to be seen. I may be here for weeks or even months. Please do not worry about me for worrying only makes one old.

There is only one thing that will ever keep me away from you and that is when I quit breathing. I know as well as my name is Ray that I will never give you up without a fight. Let me say there is a bond between us that will last into eternity. My heart is in your keeping and I will love you as long as there is breath in me.

I showed your picture to all the guys in the barracks. S/Sgt Mac Nair certainly likes you and asked why we didn't get married. I told him all I needed was the chance. In fact if I can make arrangements that is what I want to do. As it is I know that you are all mine but I would rather have the license. Just to know that you were my wife would make me the happiest man on earth. As I find it, the feeling that I get just thinking of you is a grand feeling that no one knows but lovers. As for me, all I have or ever expect to have is yours. My love is yours and there isn't a chance for another to have any of it.

P.S. Darling: I may make the call from camp. If I am able to make the arrangements tomorrow you are to meet me at New Brunswick at the Roger Smith Hotel. I will meet you Saturday morning. Please do not mention the location over the phone that I am to meet you. It may get me in trouble if you were so much as to mention New Brunswick.

Darling, I know that is what you want and so do I. I would rather address my letters to my wife than to just mention your name. "Mrs. Ruth Methvin" sounds better doesn't it?

Your loving to be husband, Ray M.

Dad arranged the furlough and mother arranged to meet him. They were married before a chaplain in the presence of two witnesses on June 8, 1943, at an Army Air Force chapel at Camp Kilmer, New Brunswick, New Jersey.

Two weeks later, on June 24, 1943, Dad left the United States on the Queen Mary. As he crossed the Atlantic he watched schools of dolphins and saw whales and gazed at the stars before falling asleep. His "bunk" was in an old drained swimming pool on deck, because the ship was so crowded with soldiers. Each man was issued a twelve-by-four-foot space to sleep. Some soldiers stuck others with safety pins to get them to vacate their bunks to make more room.

As Dad stood on the deck with the salt air blowing in his face, he would close his eyes and relive the short but happy furlough he had spent with his new bride. He was unable to share his trip across the Atlantic with her because of security regulations, but after the war he could tell Ruth: "She traveled about thirty knots and out ran every boat on the ocean, so we did not need convoy protection. It took only five and a half days to make the trip. After docking, I remained on her for twenty-four hours. From the time she docked, the troops started unloading and were still getting off when I left there. I was told that it took thirty-six special trains to carry all the troops to various parts of England. Believe me, that ship was well named. It is almost unbelievable to try and imagine how large she was. Three of us got a little mixed up on our location, and it took us over an hour to find our bunks. I will always remember her beauty and speed. I enjoyed my trip across, especially after talking with other soldiers who spent thirty days coming across in convoy."

When he arrived in Edinburgh, Scotland, Ray was sent to an Air Force base in Atcham, England. During his time overseas he was the head of all transit aircraft in Atcham, and Dijon, France. He pre-flighted American and English planes and worked shifts as long as twenty-four to thirty-six hours. When he slept, it was usually after midnight. With his heavy work hours, he got four meal tickets a day instead of the usual three.

The following are a sampling of his letters to his new wife from overseas:

July 9, 1943

My Darling wife, just a few lines to tell you that I arrived safe in England. I had a good voyage across the ocean. Coming over, I closed my eyes and relived some of the happy days we spent together. What a treasure your love has turned out to be for I know this has helped in making me a better man. Yesterday, we were married a month and ended up thousands of miles apart. We just have to make the best of it. Our day will come. Remember that I love you and that is something that never will change.

No doubt that you heard that I came across on the Queen Mary. We passed up convoys going in the same direction as if they were standing still.

I was mighty happy that I left the U.S. knowing you were mine. I am the happiest man on earth. I have never had one regret for I know that the days we were together were the happiest ones of my life. It's no wonder I worship the ground you walk on.

England is a beautiful country; everything is so green. There are lots of wildflowers to add to its beauty. It is so peaceful here the one would think that he was in the U.S. The living conditions are a lot better than I had back in the states. The food is exceptionally good; in fact the best that I have had in the army.

I visited an English town night before last. I filled my pockets with candy and gum and didn't have any trouble emptying them. In fact, I enjoyed seeing the children eat the candy and chew the gum. The expressions on their faces were my reward. One small boy who was about three years old insisted on eating the gum and I just couldn't get him to chew it. He was a cute child and I got several laughs out of him. The children here seldom get candy and they appreciate it a lot more than the children back home. In fact, I know where most of the candy I get is going. We are only allowed a small amount of candy each week.

I found the English people all friendly. In fact, I get a kick out of talking to them for they have a lingo all of their own. The English people are a lot more polite than most of we Americans. I find the English people a proud race and they have the right to be proud after all they have been through.

I am thankful that you have got a home like Aunt Mina and Uncle Watson give you. In fact, I need never worry about you as long as you are with them. I would rather think of you as being on the farm with them than any place I know.

Remember that I love you and it is nothing that will ever change.

Your loving husband, Ray

Jan 1, 1944 England

Darling Ruth,

Just thinking how wonderful it would be to be there with you. Today is the starting of a new year which I hope will bring an end to this war. Probably you are at the farm and having a big time there I hope. The holidays are over and now you will be back to teaching. Wish that I were one of your students. I know that you would more than earn your money. Probably you would wonder why you ever took up teaching.

You ask me if time goes by fast or slow. Time for me goes fast because I am busy most of the time. But to be honest it seems like I have been gone a long time. I hope that another year will see me home because I am getting fed up with this army life. I like my job but I like to be a free man to go and do as I wish. In fact I am like some little school boy impatient for school to let out for summer vacation.

As time goes on I find myself loving you all the more. I have got a lot to be thankful for. At one time I considered that I didn't stand a chance to mean much to you. Then when it did happen it all took so fast I was afraid I would wake up and find it a dream. At times I wonder just what it is that causes a person to love so strongly that no other could even substitute. Even that one person dominates night and day and I have had dreams, I am always meeting you and seeing and hearing you chuckle. It is grand to dream because you are with me and rather disappointing to wake up and find you gone.

I received a grand letter from Aunt Mina. The only thing she has against me is that I am taking you away from the East back to the West. I know that she would like to keep you there but still I know that she in a way will be glad because we two will be together again which will mean happiness for both of us. Aunt Mina understands but from what she stated in her letter she hates to see you leave. The only hurry that I am now in is to get back where you are. The only thing that is holding me is a war which seems to just drag on and on as the days drag into months . . . it seems years since I last saw you.

I was just thinking about the times we had together. From the first day I started going with you there has always been problems which limited our being together. At first it was school and what Mother would say if you were out too late or out too many times in a week. Then again it was more school or my going North. Today it is a war and me being a soldier which is the only thing that is keeping us separated. I am going to say that after this war is over that hell and high water isn't going to keep me away this time. The way I feel now is that there wouldn't be anything more pleasing to the touch than an armful of you.

Darling there is nothing I would like better than to spend Christmas with you. In fact it is out of the question to ever consider a good Christmas unless you are with me. There is no use faking something when your thoughts are ten thousand miles away. When day comes for me to return it is going to be one of the happiest days of my life.

Your loving husband, Ray

Feb 28, 1944

Dearest Sweetheart,

Received three letters which as you should know made me happy. In fact a letter from you is all that is needed to make a perfect day.

Tonight I am C.Q. a job I dislike but nevertheless have to do it. I am still in the best of health. If I felt any better, I just couldn't stand it.

On my twenty-four hour pass last week the most outstanding event was an English boy who came up to the bus and asked for some American chewing gum. Every soldier that he asked gave him the answer "No." Finally he ups and said, "It is bleeding strange than none of you Yanks has any gum for after all most of the American Army must be here." We all had a good laugh and the little fellow ended up getting his gum.

At times I wonder about the small part I am playing in winning this war. I think about the boys that are fighting in Italy and in the jungles of the South Pacific through all kinds of weather and facing death most of the time. I guess you for one could say that I am lucky. I know that I have got three good meals a day coming and a warm bed to sleep in. I have never had any occasion to face any dangers and have never been deprived of a lot that others have. About the only thing that I gave up was my home life. The job I have been given to do I do to the best of my ability.

It seems rather foolish to try and write a letter and not be able to state what towns and cities I visited on my furlough. I never stayed too long in any one place. I enjoyed my trip after a fashion. To be honest it wasn't as grand a furlough as the one last year. This place I was among strangers with no place in general to go. At the end of seven days I was glad to get back to the base. It is going to be some time before I ask for another one. I discovered that I can visit hundreds of places and be free to go at will but without a certain person's company the trip will never be what it should. Now say for instance, if you had been with me it would have been a grand trip.

It does me good to get away from the base and mingle with the English people. From what I gather from talking to them I can now appreciate my country a lot more. Now I have come to the conclusion that I come from one of the grandest countries in the world. It has taken this war to make me appreciate my county the way that any good citizen should and let me say that I, for one, am proud that I come from the good ole U.S.A. I like our government because it comes closer to being a government for the people and by the people.

I saw a lot of Negro soldiers making love to English girls. Most of the girls think they are American Indians and find them fascinating. A lot of white yanks do not like the idea of Negroes going with white girls and there has been lots of fights and a few killed.

How anxious I am right now to return back home to you. Whenever the day comes for me to get on the boat to return will be a happy day because I know it will mean seeing you again. I am proud of my wife and rather anxious to take her back and show her off to my people.

If you decide to teach another year that will be O.K. by me. In my estimation the war is not going to end this year. You will find me reasonable regardless of what you choose to do. I would be more than willing to wait until you were free. No doubt I could help Harold or Uncle Watson. Then again I would even consider keeping house for you. "Ha." Who knows I may even make a good cook. It would be fun to keep house and cook for you providing that you are willing to live under can opener conditions.

Darling, I appreciate your asking me such questions. For me to decide what is best is hard to do at this time. It is up to you to decide what you wish to work at. I can make suggestions but after all I would rather you be the one to decide and not me. Whatever will make you happy is good enough for me.

Your letters sound like you miss me as much as I miss you. I find the going a lot easier because I know I have someone grand to return home to. Confidentially I may be a soldier but my heart is with you. How I do hope that this war will end because I am tired of being a soldier.

You asked me how old Rondel is. There is only a little over a years difference in the ages of we boys. Rondel's hair started turning gray in high school. It doesn't seem believable that his hair is gray when there isn't a gray hair in my head.

Last night I was Charge of Quarters or C.Q. I didn't get much sleep as I was up most of the night awaking men for detail or duty. The C.Q. has numerous duties such as checking blackout violations and correcting them. The C.Q. is held responsible for all disorders and it is his duty to stop and break them up. I had forty-two men to get up during the night. I only got four hours sleep but it was well worth it because I was again with you. The alarm clock interrupted the dream but probably some other time I will know the true end of it. There is so much noise during the day that I cannot sleep. I would like to have had a little more shut-eye.

I am more than anxious to leave here and come back home where I can start to live again. How grand it is going to be to be free and to go and do whenever you wish. Starting out and planning our lives together is going to be a pleasure that I have dreamed about for a long long time.

The speech that you gave on fabrics to the B & P Women's Club no doubt was interesting to them. I was thinking that it would be about as interesting to me as a talk I would make on some part of an airplane to you.

Received two of your letters and had a good laugh over some of them. How well I remember the time that the officer insisted on me moving my car but I was intoxicated with love and just couldn't be bothered. Today I am glad that we kept our love on the up and up. I have known you a good many years and I trust you because I know the kind of life you have led.

You mentioned about the time I kissed you goodnight and when I reached for the door it was open with your mother standing in it! How well I remember that time for I was almost afraid to come back for fear that she would show me the door.

Some of these days we are going to be together again and have a lot of good times.

Goodnight, Darling, and pleasant dreams. I am rather anxious to collect all those kisses that you have saved up for me.

Always your lover, Ray

May 25, 1944

My Darling Wife:

Wednesday I got a pass starting at noon and ending at one that night. I went cycling the long way to town. I made a trip of about twenty miles to get six. In fact I visited several small towns that I had never been in. Everything is so green over here. The flowers are just starting to bloom. England with its rolling hills carpeted with grass is a beautiful country. I couldn't help marveling at the beauty as I cycled along the narrow roads. My thoughts were thousands of miles away and I just couldn't help wishing that I was home with you. What a perfect day it would have been if you had of been here.

I rather think that no matter what I may go through that I will be the same person when I get back as when I left. I do believe that there isn't a man in the army that hates army life any more than I do. Yet, I realize the easiest way to get along with the army is to be a good soldier. I have never had any trouble or been in trouble and what's more I am going to come out of this army with a good record. I have always made the best of whatever the army gave me to do. I find my work interesting and consider that I am lucky to be in the place that I am. I know that regardless of what is to come that I will make the best of it and will not let anything get me down.

Honey, I do hope you get a job that you like. I would like to receive a letter stating that you were going to teach another year at Beverly. But I would be like you when it comes to signing a contract, like was offered to you. Whatever you do will meet my approval as long as I hold your love.

I need you as much now as if I were living with you. I wish I could lay my head in your arms tonight and go to sleep on my private pillow. That would be the next thing to heaven. I wish I were there so I could love you and catch up on a lot that I have lost.

Tonight I am C.Q., a job that I can be honest in saying that I rather dislike. But I am no better than anyone else so I am willing to take my turn.

Today is our wedding anniversary which I shall not fail to mention. I shall never forget how happy you looked and the tears of joy that you shed when you were pronounced Mrs. Methvin by Chaplin Drumheller. I know that I too looked like I was about to explode with happiness. For the first time in my life I felt that I was alive, living in a wonderful world. It actually felt that I had never lived up until that one day. At that time I made a solemn promise that I would never do anything to bring disgrace upon you and that I would do everything in my power to make you happy and proud of me. I shall never gamble my happiness away as some men do because I know where my greatest happiness lies. I only hope that you will say that I have lived up to theses vows. True, I realize we have been parted the greater part of our first year; but at that I have never stopped loving you. I have never had room to doubt you and I trust you regardless of our long separation because I know that our love is made of the strongest stuff.

Now that the second front has started I am glad because I can now see the beginning of the end of the war for the Germans. Before it seemed the war was going on with no end in sight. We all have high hopes in our success for victory. I hope that it is over before the New Year begins. I am more than ready to start home and start living my life with you. I hope that I get the opportunity to spend the next wedding anniversary with you. What a celebration that is going to call for!

Wednesday I was in town on pass and checked on the snap shots. The reprints weren't ready and I was told to come back next week. I didn't stay all night at the R.C.C. but I do know that I fell asleep in a good soft chair. It is good to be able to relax and forget that you are alive in a nice soft chair.

Honey, I think that you have done a good job building up a bank account. I never dreamed we had that much in the bank. In fact I never bothered to keep track of the money I sent you for I knew that you were a good manager. In fact, you shall always be my banker. I hope we will be able to pay for a home when I get out of this army. I can hardly wait for this war to end.

I had a grand dream last night. I am thankful that we were gifted with the power to dream. Its odd just how close a dream can bring out an object or person and then when awakened one has to shake his head almost in doubt.

Always your lover, Ray

England

June 26, 1944

The news sounds good and if we keep going like we have in the past month this war cannot last much longer. If the Allies keep going like they have it shouldn't be long until victory. I doubt if the Germans can hold out much longer. This year will probably be the end for them. It will take only about another year to finish the Japs. The end will not come too soon for me. I hope that I can catch the first boat home. In fact, I have lost out on a lot of loving and it will take years to catch up. See what you are in for when I get home?

Received your grand letter on the 13th. To be honest, I am glad that you are going to teach in Beverly again and will be living close to Aunt Mina and Uncle Watson on the Walker Plantation. For my part, someday I hope I can repay them for all they have done for you. No doubt you are again settled at the farm. Under all probability there is plenty of work to do. I have never seen a farm that one couldn't find plenty to do. I have spent some rather long hours working on them and at the end of the day had little to show for my work. To be honest I wish I could spend a month this summer there with you.

I am well pleased with your decision to visit your sister Helen and Chet in Bend. Someday we are going to make the same trip together and what a grand time we are going to have.

Received the package in good shape. I only got one piece of fudge but it was good. Too many hungry boys in the barracks.

Give my love and Darling keep most of it for yourself.

Your loving husband, Ray M.

Jan 3, 1945

Hello Darling,

I am rather starting the New Year off poorly when it comes to writing you a letter. I was intending to write this letter on the first day of the year. I spent rather an odd New Year's Day working on an airplane at an English base. The plane had an emergency landing and the S/Sgt Jerozal and I were sent to make repairs.

This is a day worth mentioning because it happens to be my third anniversary in the army. Starting today I get longevity pay which will amount to $4.80 a month.

It has been ages since I heard from Mother. I write now and then but nothing like I should. Last year I only recall receiving two letters from her. It is rather hard to write letters to a person and never receive one. Mother is getting rather old and I guess I had better overlook it and write more often.

Today I moved into a room with S/Sgt Jerozal. Believe me it seems good to be in a room with only two of us after being out in the barracks with twenty-six. Some of the boys get a little lit up at times and wake everyone up which never did set too well with me. The walls are covered with pin-up girls but you happen to be my favorite for I have your picture on my shelf.

Everything is so uncertain. I may be here today and gone tomorrow but only time will tell that.

I get to thinking about the length of time that I have known you before we even thought or considered getting together. I shall always remember the grand time we had together in California and how your mother used to worry about me taking you away from her. I have to laugh when I think about the first time you ever drove a car and how excited you got whenever you wanted to stop and then again when you wanted to start the car in motion. What I remember most is that when it came to loving you, you would only go so far and then put your foot down and tell me off. It is such memories as those that make me today trust, admire, and love you.

Give all my love and I wish I could crawl up into your arms and go to sleep. Goodnight, Darling, and God bless you.

Your loving husband, Ray

England

Feb 6, 1945,

Tonight is one of those lonely nights; for I am in the barracks all alone. There used to be twenty-eight and now there are only two of us left. Jerozal is away and I shall have the barracks to myself tonight. It rather seems odd that everything is so peaceful and quiet. If a sparrow were to fly over and chirp it would sound like a fire siren.

Wednesday night I was out with Jerozal and Mac pubbing. I tried to keep up with them drink for drink but ended up by being good and sick. I guess I was never cut out to be a drinking man. What's more, I have no intentions of becoming one. That is one thing I am not going to do when we are together. Honey, I shall never let my home be broken up by drinking.

The A.R.C. [American Red Cross] offers the warmest and most homelike place that a soldier can find. I for one will give the A.R.C. a lot of credit for what they are doing for the boys over here. You mentioned something about wanting me to spend a night at a good hotel while on furlough. I tried to get a room at a good hotel but discovered that there were no rooms to be had. Another Sgt. and myself took the room unsight and unseen. The room cost one pound. We both were tired and we just got into bed not paying much attention to the condition that the bed was in. The lights shining on the sheets made them look white. In the morning, a maid brought tea and toast for breakfast and served it to us in bed. After eating, I noticed the sheets and they had the appearance that a dozen or more people had slept in them. What I mean is they were dirty. I called my discovery to the attention of the sergeant. I know from what he said the same feeling ran through him that did me. All that we wanted to do was get out and go to a town where there was a good A.R.C. and take a bath. In fact, it didn't take either one of us long to get out of town.

I will admit there are lots of women that are out looking for the American soldier, but the wrong kind. Most cases it is his money and not the soldier that she is after. He is rather a big fool if he caters to her because he is making a big gamble on his health and life's happiness. I had a lot of chances to step out on you while in London. In fact it is hard to walk down the street at night without being propositioned. The kind that want money are in my estimation, more deadly than bullets. I think too much of my health and too much of you ever to take that chance. I couldn't find your equal and ended up being true. I know that my happiness is with you. I am not going to gamble my happiness away on some streetwalker. I believe the road to happiness is having just one and trying to make her happy. No one could take your place even for a day. I have a lot of grand memories of my wife which will be lived and relived and keep me from even considering such things.

There isn't too much more to write about unless I mention the fact that I am still madly in love with you.

I find loving you my greatest pleasure.

Love, Ray

England

March 17, 1945

My Darling Wife:
The valentine was exceptionally good. Today is another anniversary day spent apart. Even so, there is a lot of grand memories. From all indications, Sweetheart, it would take

an act of God if we were together on the 8th of June. Regardless of where I may be, I can be honest in saying that I have been a lot happier knowing that you are my wife than if I could only count you as a dear girl friend. Today, at times I wonder what is in the makeup of a man to make him only love one person when there are thousands of others.

I took a twenty-four hour pass on my birthday. I had full intentions of celebrating the occasion by getting slightly drunk. I made a rather feeble attempt and gave it up as a bad job. I took in a picture show and saw Old Oklahoma. Nothing short of being a Wild West show.

I see no harm in mentioning that I got to see a little of Paris. In fact we were lost and drove around for miles before finding our way out. The people were very friendly because they waved and greeted us with a smile. I saw some of the damndest headgears on women. The people seem rather friendly here but I am not able to talk to them. It is rather hard to learn French out of a book because I fail to pronounce the word properly and they cannot understand me. I even failed miserably at trying to talk in sign language. The small children know a few words of English. Just enough to ask for gum, candy, and cigarettes.

Probably I will not get any more mail from you for some time to come. I have been living the life of a gypsy the past week. I doubt if I will ever be able to eat another C ration. I drove a vehicle over a thousand miles. At one time I was near the German border. I stayed there only a day and left for Southern France. I never realized just what it would be like to be in a country that talked another language. Even the dogs here do not understand my lingo. The French just look at me and say, "I no comprendo" and shrug their shoulders.

It has been several days since I last wrote. I am now settled down and will probably be here several months. The climate is about the same as in California. I like the climate a lot better here than in England.

To be honest I know little about the French people. But from what I have seen and what little dealings I have had with them I will never undertake to understand them. I realize that I am handicapped because I am unable to speak their language.

The squadron I am now in gave a party for the French. I got rather amused because the G.I. was left out in the cold. The French danced with one another but few with the Americans. The French girls danced with their French boyfriends but refused to dance with the Americans. At no time did I see more than four Americans dancing.

I thought that the prices were high in England but nothing like they are here. Inflation has made the French franc not worth much. In fact, a soldier's money doesn't go far here. I doubt if I will care much to go to town. There isn't anything to go to town for beings as how I am unable to speak French.

I am now living in a tent with four others. Some days I am rather busy while other days I have little to do. I would rather stay at the base than go to town. There is no advantage in drinking at a bar and trying to talk sign language and make the people understand what you wish.

The news certainly looks good and if the allies keep going like they have in the past few days it shouldn't be too long until this war is over. Then I hope that I get to come home for awhile before going to the Pacific. Great life, this being a soldier.

It seems ages since I last saw you and I realize that life today would be rather empty if it were not for you. I will write another V-mail tomorrow.

Love, Ray

Dijon, France

March 27, 1945

Hello Honey:

Just a short letter to let you know that I am still in circulation and thinking mostly of you. I have given up the idea of coming home. It seems that it has been ages since I last saw you. It looks like I am going to be in the army of occupation. If that is to be my luck, I would gladly trade places with one who didn't want to go to the Pacific. Providing that I would get a month furlough in the United States. I am ready for anything, providing that I get to come back home. Honey, I am starved for love and my private pillow. The trouble with me is that only one can fill the bill when it comes to dishing out love. You have spoiled me for I have lost interest in the fair sex. What I need right now is a lot of your loving; that would certainly do me a lot of good.

My Thunderbolt had a flat tire over in Germany today and I may be lucky and fly over tomorrow and fix it. At least I was hoping that I get the chance. I got a little aggravated yesterday because they took me off a Thunderbolt that I got up in good shape and put me on another that was war weary. I expect to have the old wreck in good shape in a couple of weeks.

All that I might write would never be able to express in words just how much I still love you.

Give my regards to all, Ray

France

April 10,1945

Hello Sweetheart,

I thought about you on our anniversary day but wasn't able to write. V-E Day I was enrouted in convoy and spent the night at Leon. The people of Leon went wild and I would say really celebrated the occasion. Large groups of French went down the street singing the Mariellaise and the

Madelon. I would say that the American soldiers took the news rather calmly and none that I saw went on a spree. The day was more a celebration for the French than for us, for to them the war is over. We've got the first half of the war over but the second is coming up and it was beyond me to get in the mood to celebrate. I even had French women come up and throw their arms around me and kiss me on the cheek. The most amazing thing that I saw was men kiss one another which to me seemed rather out of place. Probably if I understood French the celebration would have meant more. Say for instance, if I could have been with you that celebration would have meant more to me.

Thank you for the gum and the candy. I should have enough gum to last for a long time. I know that it will make a lot of French children happy.

About the only recreation I have is a picture show. Most of the pictures are old pictures that I have seen back in the states about four years ago. Last night they showed the picture, "She's a Soldier Too" starring Beulah Bondi and Nina Foch.

Honey, you keep bringing up Aunt Mina wanting us to stay in the East but I have never gotten your opinion. It appears to me that we should decide the issue together. To be honest, I have no idea of what I am going to do after this war is over. Time will tell but my problem now is to get out of this army and become a civilian. The way things look that will be several years from now and the way I see it now is to make the best of it. I am fed up with the army life but still I know and realize that the only thing to do is not to let this army life get the better of me. I have to see it through and when I am given my freedom I am going to be the happiest person on earth. I have got you to love and work for and that will always mean a lot to me.

I still say that I am a lucky fellow to have you for a wife.

Yours alone, Ray

April 16, 1945

Hello Honey,

Just a few lines to let you know that I am enjoying the best of health. For the past week I have been helping make an engine change. There certainly is a lot of work attached to it. Now that most the work is finished on the plane I will be able to take it easy for a few days.

V-mail is about the only mail going through. Once in a while I receive an air-mail that makes good time and again it takes over a month.

Honey, I would rather have you decide the question of where we are going to live because everything is so uncertain. Would you rather live in the East or the West? Regardless of which you choose, let me know your reason.

I am glad you had a good time in New York. I wish that I had been there to meet you at the railroad station as I have done in the past. It is a grand sight to see you coming and a grand feeling to hold you knowing you were mine.

In a few days I will have some snap shots for you. By the way I shall take a picture or make an attempt of some of these French women so I can show you what their hats look like and the way they do their hair. I stand a good chance of getting my face slapped but nevertheless it will be worth the chance.

Sgt. Murray is in the same tent with me. From what the Stars and Stripes articles that I have read says that most all of the Air Corps will not be discharged but will be moved to the Pacific. Some will go to the US while others will go directly to the Pacific without leaves. Those going to the US will probably get a thirty day leave. I hope that I will be one of the lucky ones. There is a good chance that I will, as well of thousands of others be disappointed.

It is getting late so I guess that I had better sign off because it is about bed time.

It is a pleasure to belong to you and I would love to be there so that you could have all of me.

Yours alone, Ray

France

May 3, 1945

You stated that you would rather live in Southern California. I will be honest in saying that I like the West better than the East. I do not know just where we will settle, for lot depends on the conditions after the war. It is rather hard to make plans especially after being in the army three and a half years. My biggest problem now is to get an honorable discharge and get out of this army. I am anxious to get this army life over and be able to live with you as a civilian. It is going to be grand to plan our home together.

The next few months will decide if I get to come home or go directly to the Pacific. I would have had a better chance of coming home sooner if I had remained in England. The war here in Europe is just about over and probably will not last over a week.

Honey, I had a grand dream last night for I was with you. Probably my dream will come true and we will be together in a few months.

Yours alone, Ray

Dijon, France

May 12, 1945

Honey, I know that beings as how this year in Europe has ended it has caused me to be rather homesick. If I get to come home and see you before going to the Pacific I will not mind going there half as much. I consider that I have been away from home long enough. You mean as much to me today as you ever did and to have anything happen that would cause us to break up would be rather hard to take. I never worry about that because I know you will be there waiting for me to come home.

I can say that I have never in all my life felt like a foreigner until I came to France. It is funny thing not being able to speak French. In England I enjoyed talking to the people and they were nice to me. I would say that I would rather have one good Englishman as a friend than a dozen Frenchmen. About the only time I saw the French smiling was on V-E Day.

I am now crewing a Thunderbolt which isn't in too good of shape. But I expect to have her in tip top condition within a months time.

Some day I know that we are going to have a lot of happiness together,

Love, Ray

Dijon, France

May 17, 1945

Dearest Ruth:

The mail has been coming through in record time here in the last month. The one airmail letter came through in six days which is a record.

According to an article in the Stars and Stripes a total of 85 points will not be enough to get out of the Air Corps. They are working on a new point system for the Air Corp.

I shall remain a soldier as long as the Japs last and I might add that I have no choice in the matter. The only logical thing I can do is make the best of it. I am just as anxious to see you as when I was looking for you to come in on the train at Grand Central Railway Station at New York City.

You asked me about the hotels and restaurants in Marseille. All restaurants are off limits to American soldiers as well as hotels that are not operated by the US Government. The only eats that I got were a few snacks at the A.R.C. which wasn't much.

As far as you coming to France that is out of the question.

I still say that I dislike Dijon. The people are not friendly and in my estimation rather look down on us. It is seldom one ever sees a smile. I wonder if they would rather the Germans had stayed.

I went on pass to Dijon. The thing that I like to do the most is eat at G.I Joes. There is an orchestra that plays American songs and it gives one the opportunity to forget that he is a soldier.

In England the little children came up and begged for candy and gum which always pleased me because it showed that they were friendly and wanted something that I had to offer. Just seeing the pleasure on their little faces was my reward. I got a little kick out of giving it to them because every time they saw me they smiled and I knew that I had a little friend.

Thursday I was in town most the day. I did a lot of walking and passed hundreds of children and there wasn't one of them that asked me for a stick of gum. It appeared that they didn't want anything to do with any Yank.

Give my regards to all.

Love, Ray

Dijon, France

May 31, 1945

Hello Honey,

Just a short letter to let you know my thoughts are of you. My biggest job now is to become a civilian. I get a big kick out of thinking about where we are going to decide to live and the home that we are going to own. I am pleased that you decided you would rather go West.

Again I was confronted with the problem of doing a small washing. To cope with the problem it took only one package of cigarettes, a bar of laundry soap, six candy bars, and two packages of gum to do the trick. I got a French woman to do the washing. I first tried to give her money but she requested sweets, cigarettes, and soap. The French appear to have plenty of money but nothing to spend it on.

Again it is pouring rain and water is starting running underneath my cot. I have got both of my barracks bags on the highest ground in the tent. One good thing is that the ground is naturally gravelly. Otherwise it would be rather muddy. I am going to find another place for my bags. E-gods where am I going to put them? I now have them on the bed; let it rain. I have my feet on the ground and there is a good half inch of water running around my shoes.

Honey, I am beginning to wonder just what it would be like to live in a house once more. At times I get rather fed up with this life and would give most anything to get away from it. It is beyond me how any man can become a professional soldier. To be honest there is nothing like being a civilian and being able to be king of yourself. It looks as if I am going to have to put in the best years of my life in the army. What rather gets my goat is that I do not know how many more I am going to have to endure. Just knowing that the war with Germany is over and still remaining at doubts as to what I am going to do or where I am going next makes me good and homesick.

I would be the happiest man in the world if I could come home to you if even for a short time. An armful of you would boost my moral a lot.

I see today in the Stars and Stripes where Andrew J. May, Chairman of the House Military Committee today called for a discharge of all soldiers over 35 except for key men. I have just passed that mark. If the bill goes through I am going to do my best to get a discharge.

I am helping make an engine change on a B-26. My Thunderbolt is up in the air. I am supposed to have a day off but I see from all the work that is piled up I will spend it working. Some of the boys in the squadron are not doing much work while others have more than they can do.

There isn't much to write about but I got started and rather fooled myself.

As long as I hold your love that is all that matters regardless of the time the war holds us apart.

I will try to drop you another line in a few days.

Yours forever and ever, Ray

Dijon, France

June 5, 1945

Just received your letter and was glad to receive it.

In my estimation the Jap war cannot last over a year and a half. The Japs have lost control of the air as well as the sea and those are two big factors in winning a war. Whenever our combined air might get into position, the Japs have had it. It was the Air Force that gave Germany the knockout punch and the same fate is now in store for Japan.

The one disadvantage we had at the start of the war with Japan and Germany was that we had a small Air Force and Army to defend ourselves. That took some time to build up to its present strength. Now that we have a large Army, Navy, and Air Force just how long will Japan stand up under the pounding that she bargained for? Japan knows that she has lost the war but it is only fighting on in hopes of getting an honorable peace other than unconditional surrender.

You ask me what I was going to do now that the war is over. I am working as hard now as when the war was going on. Whenever I am not crewing a Thunderbolt P47 I am either working on a B25, B26, or a C47.

I know that you will be rather anxious to know what is going to happen to me. The rumors are flying rather fast and furious and in close formation. First we are going to come home. Then another rumor will come out that we are going directly to the Pacific.

I have heard that my mail will be censored in the squadron I am moving to and that my APO number will be changing. I do know that all of us will be going into several different squadrons. When I find up just what the set up is going to be I will let you know.

I am still working for the 42 Bomb Wing.

I get so fed up with this army life but common sense tells me that there is only one thing to do and that is to make the best of it. The only kind of discharge I want is an honorable one. The day I become a civilian is going to be the happiest day of my life. Then I know that we will be able to live our lives the way we choose. Wouldn't it be a lot of fun planning our home?

The only thing that I am happy about is that I have got you for a wife even though I might have to put in thirty years in the Army.

I am in love with you today as much as when I left. I never expect to get over it either. Good night, Darling, and pleasant dreams.

Yours alone, Ray

Dijon, France

June 8, 1945

Hello Darling,

Two years have passed and I was hoping we could celebrate our anniversary together. Gee! What I wouldn't give to be with you tonight to celebrate our second anniversary. I can honestly say that my love for you remains unchanged. I have received a lot of joy and happiness just thinking about you and knowing that you will be there to greet me whenever I do get to come home. Having you has made me a better person because if I had of been free I would have probably done as the majority of soldiers are doing today, and that is going with any old skirt that looks at them. A lot of them have paid a price for their fun because they have ended up with venereal disease. From what has happened in our squadron, I am glad that I have lived the life I have because in the end I will be clean as well as money ahead.

Honey, to be honest with you the army life is rather cruel. It separates you from your home and loved ones. I cannot say that I am enjoying life because I have to do what I am told and cannot do as I wish. From the start until the finish I can say that I hate being a soldier. I never was made for a soldier because I like the civilian life better. It would be grand to have a home of our own and not to have to be always on the move. Especially to have freedom to do as you wish and to be able to live your own life. It would be a change to decide what you most wished to do instead of doing what you are told. I will be so happy when this mess is over and I can be with you.

Today I got to see what class I am in. I am class "A" which means that I am eligible for Pacific duty. That's what I get for having such good health. The class was judged from the soldier's medical record. I have only missed one day of duty on account of my health in three and one-half years since being in the army. I am either lucky or in one sense of the word "unlucky" I know now that I shall see the Pacific.

I had my home address changed on my service record so that when I get discharged that I will be discharged on the East coast.

I probably sound homesick, which I am and I am not ashamed to admit it. But since the European war has ended it has caused me to be more so.

The squadron is still together but will start breaking up most any day. I have no idea as to where I am going or what my chances are to come back home. At times my hopes are high and then I hear a rumor and my hopes go way down.

I have to pull a twenty-five hour inspection on my Thunderbolt tomorrow so I will be good and busy because there is a lot of work in pulling an inspection.

There is no one like you in my estimation. It is getting late and is my bedtime so I will close hoping you are in my dreams.

> *Forever and ever yours,*
> *Love, Ray*

Due to security regulations, Dad couldn't tell my mother why he was depressed. He couldn't tell her that he was on a ship headed to the Pacific in a special convoy as the only airplane mechanic. All the other men from his unit were to be discharged to return home except him. But when the war with the Japanese ended, his ship turned around and headed back to the United States. Dad arrived at Fort Divan, Massachusetts, on August 26, 1945, on the General Bliss, the ship that was originally taking him to the Pacific. He received his honorary discharge in September, and Mother was waiting for him. Finally, after two and a half years apart, they could be together.

Almost five years after enlisting in the military, my dad was free to do as he pleased. For the first time in two and a half years of marriage, my parent's time together was unrestricted, and they were able to establish a home together. They returned to Boston, where my mother had lived during the war. She continued teaching home economics. My dad worked in Uncle Watson's car dealership as his right-hand man.

Cars were hard to come by in the days following the war because fewer cars were manufactured, and they were rationed. When my mom and dad were finally able to buy a car from Uncle's Watson's dealership, they took their long overdue honeymoon. They headed west in a new Oldsmobile. My dad was eager to show off his new bride and introduce her to his family. After meeting the Methvins in northern California, they went to Bend, Oregon to see my mother's sister's family.

When they returned to Boston from their honeymoon, my mother resigned from teaching. After a year on the East Coast, my parents decided to move to California because of better working conditions and higher pay. They bought a two-wheel trailer, packed all their possessions, covered it with a tarp, and left to start a new life in California.

*　　*　　*

I was a month old when we arrived in northern California. We moved into a white two-story apartment in Westwood, a remote mountain community. My dad returned to falling timber for the Red River Lumber Company where he had started logging sixteen years earlier at the age of twenty. We moved to Pondosa a year later, and the following year by brother William was born. Pondosa was a well-established logging camp situated between Burney Falls and Mount Shasta in northeastern California's Siskiyou County.

The redwoods do not impress me. They look no bigger to me than the huge ponderosa pines I remember as a child growing up in Pondosa. Those giant trees surrounded us like silent sentinels. They brought a sense of security. Even when the wind blew their massive branches, we were not afraid because they gave us a feeling of protection and strength. They towered over our homes, but they were not a threat. In the summer we could smell the pitch and see the new green pine needles starting to form. In the fall, needles fell to the ground and created a dense padded carpet. That's when we'd gather pinecones for holiday decorations. In the winter when the snow fell, the trees became part of a natural Christmas scene. Icicles formed and froze on the eaves of the houses; Jack Frost painted winter scenes on the windowpanes; and snow blanketed the surrounding ponderosas.

Some of the bigger ponderosa pines were 6 feet in diameter and over 150 feet tall. Everything was diminished by those trees that towered above like skyscrapers and gave the little town its name. The company that owned Pondosa was Dad's employer, the McCloud River Lumber Company. After World War II, McCloud River Lumber Company produced millions of board feet of lumber to meet the demand for new homes all over the country.

Our town was a company town. The company built Pondosa: the gray flat-roofed houses and the red steep-roofed garages and the tiny red firehouses, which were interspersed in the alleys. The houses were designed to be moved on railroad cars, so after the timber was cut at one location, the logging camp could be moved to another site.

When we moved to Pondosa, it was in the days before mechanized logging. Trees were felled by hand. My dad used a seven-foot steel crosscut saw. When he first started in the woods, he "bucked" the logs, meaning he sawed the trees that were on the ground into log lengths predetermined by the mill. Each night he would leave the saw at the saw filer's shack to be sharpened by hand. The saws were nicknamed "misery whips." They had removable wooden handles on both ends, so they could be used by one man to "single buck" or with two men to "double buck."

When my dad started falling trees, he also used a single-bitted axe designed to chop with one side and pound wedges with the other. The first step was making the undercut, a notch cut halfway into the tree, to established the direction of the fall. With those big trees, loggers sometimes pounded as many as six or seven wedges to get the tree to fall in the direction it needed to go. Occasionally and with the help of a partner, my dad felled trees that were six to seven feet in diameter. And he hollered the traditional "T-i-m-b-e-r!" to warn others to rapidly get out of the way of a tree that was about to fall. Sometimes trees could hit another tree and leave a branch or debris caught up high, and then later on, if the wind came up and when no one was expecting it, the "widow-maker" could be blown loose to crash to the ground.

After the trees were felled and the branches chopped off and bucked into log lengths, cables called chokers were hooked to the logs, and they were pulled to the landing by a crawler tractor or "cat." Then logs were loaded onto the flat railroad cars with a "steam jammer" and shipped to the mill.

"Let me tell you . . ." my dad would say as swung both arms in the air talking about his logging days, "I taught a lot of them to fall, but I never required a man to do anything that I wouldn't do. I never put a green man in a bad place. If it was dangerous, I took it."

Asked if he was ever in danger, "Heavenly day, yes! I was like a cat with nine lives. One time when I was falling, the tree started to fall and hit a snag, I heard a snap and left the saw in the cut and got out of there. The saw was smashed to smithereens, but I made it out alive."

He described another time when he and a partner were falling, "The tree hit a snag and rocked. My partner froze. The tree was coming right at him. I don't know why he wouldn't run. I had to push him out of the way, and I barely made it out of the way myself. It crashed right in back of me. Now that's kinda scary. Anyone who says they haven't had close calls is a damn liar."

My dad was nicknamed "Hungry," more as a reflection of his eagerness to work than of appetite. He always wanted to get one more tree felled before boarding the man-haul bus to leave the woods each night, just as he was hungry for more hay to stack when he was a teenager. He loved to work hard, and he loved the challenge of men against the giant trees. He worked in the woods in rain and snow until the snow was so deep the loggers couldn't get into the woods and had to wait for spring to start again. Dad entered logging show competitions, and because of his experience and strength, he had some blue ribbons to show for his effort.

Loggers earned only about eighteen to twenty dollars a day, but they worked in the beauty and challenge of the outdoors. The logging industry supplied a demand and vital need for lumber. At that time, loggers were respected and admired.

Working in the woods logging was dangerous and hard physical work that depended on men's skills and muscles. My dad hand-bucked and fell until McCullough chain saws were introduced in the 1950s, and then he carried the heavy gas-driven power saw from tree to tree until he retired in the 1970s. Loggers wore heavy black jeans, plaid shirts, suspenders, and metal-spiked caulk boots that kept them from slipping on the wet tree trunks as they bucked them into logs. There were no GorTex boots to keep their feet dry. It was men against the elements. If they wore out a pair of gloves, they could get another pair at the company store.

I'd run to greet my dad when he came home from work. I remember meeting him as he walked down the red dirt lane carrying his big thermos, metal lunch pail, and tin hat. He was tired and dirty and smelled like sweat, pine needles, dust, and pitch, but he was never too tired to hug me and swing me in the air or bend down to my level. He greeted me like I was the most important person in the world to him. Then I'd carry his lunch pail as we walked the rest of the way home.

I looked up to my dad just as I did the tall ponderosa pines in Pondosa. He was always there for me. He was not an absentee father; he was not out drinking with the single men; he was never too busy or too tired for me. He was not preoccupied or unavailable. He was not "working late at the office" or tuned into the TV or on the telephone. We had none of those in Pondosa. When he listened, he gave me his full attention and didn't interrupt. I admired and respected him. What he taught me as a child remains decades later. He had kind, dark brown eyes that seemed to sparkle when he spoke to me. He taught me that instead of feeling cheated when I got the little runty slice in the center of the orange that it was the very best piece.

My dad loved to entertain us with his stories. He told about a logger he knew who ate a dozen fried eggs for breakfast everyday. He told of flying squirrels that glided from tree to tree, with flaps of skin between their body and legs that allowed them to fly. He even brought one home to show us. He loved to tell about the bears that came around while the men were sitting on the railroad tracks eating their sack lunches. One time the loggers threw bites of their sandwiches to the bears to try to get them closer and closer to a fellow logger who had dozed off. Then they watched him wake up with a start when they yelled, "Look out! Bear!" I loved listening to his stories from the woods as much as he loved telling them.

The *Sacramento Bee* published a Christmas comic strip during the holiday season each year. I remember crawling up in my dad's lap, and he would read this Christmas comic to us before tucking us in at night. One year when we went out to get our Christmas tree, Dad helped me look until we found a very special tree, one covered with small fir cones. Dad was a family man with a big heart.

Many people ask me what it was like to grow up in a logging camp. I guess I could best sum it up by saying we had nothing, and yet we had everything. We had so much of what really matters in life that we didn't need all the material things we fill our lives with now. There was no isolation, no trying to be better than the next guy, or trying to "keep up with the Joneses." Everyone was in the same situation. We lived side by side in a logging camp divided by narrow red dirt streets with box homes, all alike except that the camp bosses had a bigger box. Everyone worked for the same company and had relatively the same pay scale.

When I look back now at how we lived, I realize how simplistic it was. Basically we had a boxy house with a flat tarpaper roof and single bare light bulbs hanging from the ceilings of the bedroom, bathroom, kitchen, and living room. Each house had two wooden planks for a walkway to the door. We had sinks with old wooden boards for countertops. We had a stove for heat in the middle of the living room. The linoleum floors were worn from use and had black pathways showing through. The rest of the floors were painted boards. Yet, we needed nothing. The rent for each house was fifteen dollars, and the electricity bill was two dollars a month. We lacked nothing. As a child, I didn't know that there were people out in the world who had more than we had.

Each house had a small, picket-fenced yard with a pulley clothes line equipped with a platform to step on to hang clothes and a cloth basket for clothes pins hanging by a wire on the line. Cars were parked in the little garages next to the yards, and no one owned more than one car, so there were no cars parked on the street. A wooden ramp led from the street to the garage.

There was no coffee shop and no need for one because the men ate breakfast at the cookhouse before they went to the woods. After the men left for work, the women met at each other's houses and gossiped over coffee while the children played or went to school. They leaned over the wooden gates and chatted or exchanged recipes on the way to get the mail. Women wore aprons to protect their dresses as they cooked and canned. Because cameras didn't have flashbulbs then, mothers carried birthday cakes out to chairs in the yard where there was enough light to take pictures.

The only real competition came on washing day. Because the laundry was hung out on the clothes lines in the yards where all could see, each woman wanted her washing bleached whiter than anyone else's in camp. Sometimes they used bluing to achieve the desired look. The windows always had to sparkle and shine, too.

What you don't see you don't miss. We had the company store in Pondosa for Beechnut gum, penny candy, or five-cent candy bars. The women could pick up household staples they needed, and the men could buy work items such as gloves. There was no drug store. If anyone needed medical care or prescriptions they went to the clinic at the company-owned hospital in McCloud about twenty-five miles away.

The company store in McCloud had clothing and household supplies. Above the old cash register was a pulley with a clip on it. An employee or family member would sign the bill for purchases, then it was clipped to the pulley and sent upstairs to the accounting department. The amount of the bill was deducted from that employee's paycheck. That's what Tennessee Ernie Ford meant when he sang "I owe my soul to the company store." We needed no hardware store because the company was responsible for any needed improvements, repairs, or paint on the houses. Things like ruffled curtains the women ordered from the Montgomery Ward catalog.

We'd drive thirty miles to McArthur to buy meat at the Crum Meat Company and, at fair time, go to the Intermountain Fair for the carnival. On one of these trips we were crossing Lake Britton, and a road crew was blasting with dynamite. The flagman told my dad to stop and stay right where he was. Dad didn't feel right about staying that near the blasting, and just after he put the car in reverse and moved, a gigantic bolder landed exactly where we had been.

The women planted flowers in the yards. I remember the columbine and the hops climbing up the walls. Wildflowers and ferns grew in the meadows and woods, usually by the creeks and streams. In the summer, we went for picnics and learned to swim and floated on boards in the icy water of Bear Creek, a mile or so down the road. The only paved road was the main road into town that forked to go to the mill and to Cheney Grant, the other small community near the railroad tracks. In the winter, we sledded down the hill coming into town on the main road—perfectly safe because there was so little traffic.

There were families of various sizes, mostly white, some of Swedish or Italian descent. The single men lived in the smallest cabins that were more like bunkhouses with only a place to sleep. The company provided toilets and showers for them in a different building. If a yard got too junky or a man moved in with someone he was not married to, the camp boss paid him a visit and told him he would have to change or move on because he was not setting a good example. There was only one phone in Pondosa, at the camp boss's house and for emergency use only. For most emergencies, you could just yell out your door and the whole town would come running.

The main road in town circled a water fountain built out of rock. Children learned to ride tricycles and bicycles around that circle. There was very little traffic, and everyone in town watched out for everyone else's kids, so we had a lot of freedom in a protected environment. The two businesses in town were a tiny post office and the small country store. Whatever we couldn't find at the Pondosa store was at the larger company store in McCloud. Pondosa had a community hall for dances, baby showers, church services, and meetings, and a one-room schoolhouse with one teacher for grades first through eighth. The high school kids rode a bus to McCloud.

For entertainment, people gathered around their radios and listened to Fibber McGee and Molly or played card games at each other's houses. After dark they drove to the dump that was just out of town and watched the big black bears scavenge and eat trash. There were no televisions, no movie theatres, no restaurants, and no malls. My mother sewed our clothes and knitted our sweaters and snow hats. She patched my dad's black work pants and darned his wool socks. I didn't know the rest of the world lived any differently.

In 1951 the snow was so deep that it reached to the rooftops instead of just to the top of the fences as usual. Food had to be carried in on the railroad tracks because the roads were so deep with snow they couldn't be plowed with the equipment they had then. Men dug pathways or tunnels to the doors of all the houses and shoveled off the roofs to keep them from collapsing from the weight of the snow.

When I look at what houses are left standing in Pondosa now, they look like shacks, but at the time, I felt I lived in a palace. I didn't notice the torn, worn linoleum, I felt loved at home and in the community and safe and secure in the tall pines. In the 1960s, most people from the camp moved to McCloud and some of the houses were dismantled. The mill burned in the 1970s, so what remains now is one house in Pondosa and one in Cheney Grant, which was near the mill. The rest of the camp has returned to nature. There are no ugly cement foundations left.

The schoolhouse still stands, boarded up, with paint peeling and windows broken. The playground was removed a few years ago. The store that sold penny candy and chewing gum is boarded up too. The community hall is silent. The sounds of women visiting at baby showers, the music at dances, and the hymns of Sunday school are gone. You can only hear the wind rustling through the trees. The post office with its old-fashioned dial boxes is a remnant of the past. Who would ever know that a hundred loggers and their families lived and worked there?

You can hear the sounds of dogs barking in the yard of the one house that is still inhabited. The railroad has been abandoned. The roads between the houses became indistinguishable when, through the years, hundreds of trees grew back. In the winter, what's left of Pondosa is covered by a blanket of snow. In the spring and summer, daffodils, sweet peas, and lilacs are all that remain of the yards. In the fall, pine needles and pinecones softly rustle to the ground. It remains a beautiful strand of timber unharmed by logging or human habitation.

We lived in Pondosa for ten years, from 1946 to1956. When my brother William was old enough for school, we moved to McArthur and my mother returned to teaching. My dad continued to work for the McCloud River Lumber Company until his retirement in 1974.

*   *   *

The banner announcing "50 Wonderful Years" spread across the front of the table set for my parent's fiftieth wedding anniversary. The sun was shining; it was a beautiful warm summer day except for the blustery gusts of wind that kept knocking over the fresh flower arrangements on the white tablecloths.

The party was held in June 1993 at the fairgrounds a block from the home my parents bought in 1956 after leaving Pondosa. Friends and family gathered to celebrate. My dad's brother Rondel was there and my mother's sister Helen and cousins, nieces, and nephews from both sides of the family. My dad's half-sister, Lillian, came from Tennessee to surprise them. They all watched as my parents entered, walking arm in arm across the lawn. My parents were a great pair, my dad in his bright-colored print shirt and gray pants; my mother in her flowered skirt and red top. They were the first in line to start the buffet, and after everyone ate, they cut the cake.

They were both beaming as their grandson Scott offered a toast, "Here's to my grandparents whose marriage has survived ten presidential offices and two wars. I admire the way they have been actively involved in the community helping people. They have worked hard for what they have and yet have taken time for families and hobbies. They get along well with others and still enjoy each other after fifty years."

They had worked hard all their lives, my father as a timber faller and my mother as a home economics teacher. They looked forward to many more years together. Life was full and life was good. It was time to enjoy the fruits of their labor from the years of sacrifice and toil. My dad's dream of owning his home had come true. They had survived the depression and lived conservatively, setting aside money for retirement. They were secure financially. They never made a phone call when a postcard would do. They hung clothes on the line instead of using the dryer. Now they had money saved. My mother had plans to travel, and my dad was content to stay home because he had had enough traveling in the service. He was happy keeping things up at home and working in his garden. Their fiftieth wedding anniversary seemed to be the summation of all their hard work. They looked forward to the future with plans to enjoy family, home, hobbies, the golden years, and each other.

As they looked back on their years together, they reflected on their marriage vows and the fact that they meant just as much to them now as when they first stood before the post chaplain at the Army Air Force chapel in Camp Kilmer, New Jersey, in 1943.

Ray meant it when he promised to love Ruth, comfort her, honor and keep her, in plenty and in want, in sickness and in health, in joy and in sorrow. He had done that. He lived it daily, "forsaking every other, cleaving to her only." He kept his vows to her during the long, lonesome years after their wedding when he was in the service, and he still continued to do so. He proved all the letters he wrote to her in the service were not lines, but lifestyle. He spent the next fifty-five years of his life doing what he promised because her happiness was what mattered to him most. It was one thing to say vows and another to live them through the difficult times. Their vows stood the test of time. They were not merely words spoken by a pretty young woman and a young healthy man.

My mother had no way of knowing that in only a year her promises to my dad would be tested by Alzheimer's as people advised her to divorce him to qualify him for Medi-Cal, so she wouldn't have to pay the high cost of his care. Those who would try to persuade her underestimated what those vows, taken over fifty years ago, meant to her. She refused to divorce him for financial reasons, just as she knew he would refuse the same.

She had no way of knowing that "in sickness and in health" would mean that he could no longer think clearly. He would no longer be able to love her, comfort her, honor, and keep her. She had no way of knowing that keeping him would be an unimaginable challenge. Yet, she meant the vows she had said, past, present, and future, unlike the woman in a doctor's office who said, "You realize doctor, my husband has lost his mind, and I can't take him back in that state."

My parent's vows were more than empty words. They reflected the same depth of commitment as the man I saw visiting his unresponsive wife in a long-term care facility. The old man had a very difficult time walking, even with a cane. He came faithfully, daily, to sit at the bed of his demented wife, even though she never even acknowledged his presence. As he bent over his wife's bed, he looked up at me and said, "I come because you don't write off sixty years of marriage just because she no longer knows who I am."

In 1956 when my mother decided to return to teaching, my parents had packed all their belongings in their two-wheel trailer and moved from Pondosa to McArthur, about fifty miles to the southeast. Mother and Dad bought a home with money they had saved and with help from the G.I. bill. My dad's life-long dream was finally realized; he had a home of his own. It was a single-story, three-bedroom house with knotty pine interior, built in the 1930s, but to my parents, it was brand new. My dad liked the location, right on the main street, because he was tired of shoveling snow. Even though he would have a hundred-mile round trip to work, he could pull directly onto the highway from his carport.

During those years when my dad was living in town and working in the woods, he would get up at four in the morning, eat a hearty breakfast of oatmeal "because it sticks with you" then load his lunch pail and metal cork-topped thermos into his Studebaker pickup. Once a week my brother walked across the street to the Crum Meat Company and picked up their standing order for a beef tongue that my mother would season and boil for my dad's lunch. Each evening my mother packed his lunch pail with an apple, homemade date cake, and a beef-tongue sandwich to give him the energy he needed to carry a heavy power saw, gas can, and axe from tree to tree.

Dad drove fifty miles to McCloud, or he met the "crummy," the man-hauling rig, at the crossroad. He worked from the time the snow melted and it was dry enough to get into the woods until winter set in again. He worked in all conditions, as long as they could get to their cutting site without getting stuck. When he came home, he had his gas tank filled at the gas pump across the street. The owner always washed his windshield, and they visited. Later, he described my dad as "one hell of a good man."

When he got home after a full day's work, Dad entered through the back door carrying his lunch pail, thermos, cork boots, and tin hat, usually just as my mother was getting home from school. His face was black from sweat clinging to the dirt that matched his thick, dark brown hair. Now he was ready to relax at their 1950s metal kitchen table and enjoy his cup of coffee with a teaspoon of honey and cream—even if it was 100 degrees outside.

Dad would discuss the day's events and dilemmas with my mother. She would tell him about her plans for an upcoming fashion show or what a particular student did during her home economics cooking class. He was an attentive listener, offering advice only when asked: "In my estimation . . ." or "Whatever you think is best, I want you to be happy." Then he would tell her something like how he wedged a tree with an axe to get it in the direction he needed it to fall. His calm demeanor, gentle spirit, and flexibility balanced my mother's drive and need to be scheduled. He had an easy peaceful nature. He didn't have to "call the shots." There was never any question about who was boss in the family: "Ruth is of course," he would say.

When he was not working in the woods in the winter, my dad rose early every morning and built up the fire, so the house would be warm for Mother when she got up after he took her coffee in bed. Then he'd spend the day working on the new addition that he built onto the house. Dad loved working in his yard whenever he could. He spent time on weekends hauling manure and lava rocks to define his flowerbeds and garden. He knew the value of hard work, and his yard and garden reflected it. He enjoyed seeing the fruits of his labor and sharing with friends and relatives. He carried in armloads and buckets full of produce that my mother canned or used to make pies. He entered his fruits and vegetables in the fair and received many first place ribbons for his efforts. He was guilty of bragging about his accomplishments. "These are the best red delicious apples in all of northern California," he'd say, but he meant well, and to him they were. People driving through town often stopped to admire his flowers.

My dad was happy working with just a shovel, rake, and wheelbarrow. He could do anything he wanted with those tools. Who could ask for more? He had no interest in modern tools or new gadgets. Whenever we would buy him a new tool for gardening he would say, "Now what in the hell did you buy me that for?"

Dad loved making arrowheads from obsidian and other stones he found in the Nevada desert. In an1983 interview in the *Mountain Echo Fair Guide* he said, "You never know what is in store for you when you begin to work on a new piece. How the rock or obsidian chips and the colors you get when you finish are a new experience to enjoy." During the winter months, he and my mother arranged his arrowheads in frames to hang in their home. He often exhibited his handiwork in competitions at the local fairs. They visited museums to get ideas for new designs, and he'd start working on them as soon as he returned home. Typical of Dad, he was always happy to oblige when asked to teach his craft to school children and the Boy Scouts. He helped Mother with her hobbies as well, by making wooden handles for the handbags she sewed.

My dad didn't desire new cars or toys for himself. He lived through the depression, and he wasted nothing. If something wore out he just found another use for it. When his metal bucket got a hole in the bottom of it he patched it with a torn strip of linoleum and filled it with kindling for the fireplace. He didn't toss it out and replace it with new. He was very conservative and willing to do without in order to save money for his daughter and grandchildren's college educations. He also used any opportunity to tear down old buildings to get the used wood. He'd say, "You never know when you might need good lumber."

An old, unoccupied school in McCloud was to be torn down after a logging truck had lost its brakes and ran into it. My dad suggested to my husband that they tear it down and salvage the lumber. Along with the school, they also tore down four houses. They pulled nails, made big stacks of boards, and then hauled the lumber fifty miles home. Dad helped my husband build a new home for us with the used lumber, and he never expected anything in return.

The only physical problems my dad had were a broken collarbone, a knee replacement, a minor prostrate surgery, and psoriasis. His psoriasis was worse at times of stress, but even though his chronic skin condition made his hands crack and bleed and the skin flake off, it never stopped him from hard physical work, and he always had a firm handshake. In spite of time spent at a treatment center, his psoriasis never went away.

My dad would sing while he worked but always the same two songs. "Songs to give Bing Crosby competition," he'd say as he sang "I'm Dreaming of a White Christmas" (summer and winter) and "Home on the Range."

When my parents bought their home in McArthur, the town was just a wide spot in the road, and it hasn't changed much since. State Highway 299 East runs through the middle of town and past the post office, church, store, fairgrounds, restaurant, bar, and garage. That's about all there is to McArthur. Businesses come and go but never spread to the outskirts of town, they just exchange places in the same location. McArthur is a place where everyone knows everyone or is related to someone who does. If a new person walks in any business, all heads turn to look. If anyone is dressed up, they look out of place. People are called by name when they enter the local store. Men have their morning coffee, bacon, eggs, and hash browns and discuss politics or the hay market at the coffee shop. At noon they come in for hamburgers and fries. Women gather at the restaurants in sweatshirts and casual clothes to have lunch and play pinochle. The waitress usually knows what someone is having before they order.

Men wear billed hats with slogans like "Get er' done" or a company name like "Carpenter's Trucking." Loggers wear torn plaid shirts, black work pants-some with suspenders-and boots. Locals drive four-wheel-drive pickups, usually with a dog in the back. Some pull horse and stock trailers. The noon whistle sounds everyday. School buses pass through hauling kids to and from school. If an emergency vehicle sounds a siren, people look out their windows or walk outside to see what direction it is going while they try to figure out who and what prompted the call. Volunteer fireman run down the road in an attempt to catch up with the fire truck as it heads out to the scene.

If kids do anything wrong, they have not only their parents but the whole town to answer to. Little incidents usually make the paper along with police reports of barking dogs and other similar disturbances. It is not uncommon to dial a wrong number and talk for a half hour because you recognize the voice. Gossip spreads like wildfire, and you don't want to get caught in its path. But on the other hand, McArthur also has the good qualities of a small town. If there is a need, everyone is there to help.

McArthur is red-neck country. In the 1960s a group of vigilante businessmen decided to "clean up the town." They held a longhaired hippie down, cut his hair, and shaved his beard. The amazing thing is that they got away with it.

McArthur has four definite seasons. In spring farmers are out in their fields getting ready to plant their first crops. Summer is a time of green and gardens, and children are out riding bikes and playing. Fall is a time of harvest and the first frost, a time of getting wood for the winter. In the winter snow, you might see cowboys on horseback driving cattle right through town, hollering as they go, with cow dogs nipping at the heels of the wayward cows.

For my parents, the 1950s and 1960s in McArthur were mostly filled with working and raising my brother and me. Life with William, my brother, was far from problem free. William was disturbed. He was loved, but he had severe behavioral problems and epilepsy. My parents disagreed on how to handle him, and that caused problems between them. My mother didn't allow my dad to discipline William, and that caused my dad great frustration and deep concern for what William might be like when he grew up. William was intelligent and took an active part in building the local museum but was unable to get along socially.

My brother came up missing in February 1966. He was sixteen years old, and I was in college. My parents were horribly distraught not knowing where he could be or what could have happened to him. There was an all points bulletin out for him, which produced leads that proved to be wrong. Someone thought he had run away to join the service instead of finishing high school. Others thought they had seen him down the highway at a big intersection, hitchhiking. My parents would get their hopes up and then have them dashed. My dad asked the fire department to go with him to search Pit One Canyon, the steep and treacherous canyon below the road between Burney and Fall River. William's whereabouts remained unknown for over a week. In the end, all leads proved futile, and there was nothing my parents could do but wait. Eight days passed, and two girls riding horseback at the fairgrounds, only a block away from our home, saw William's body lying under the bleachers where he reportedly had died of exposure. There was no foul play, and no one else was involved.

The way my parents found out that he had died was heartbreaking. Someone called the neighbors and asked them to go to my parent's house and relay the horrible news. The neighbors misunderstood and thought they were only to go and give support and comfort. While they were there, my mother looked out the window and said, "Oh look, the hearse is pulling up in front of our house." The deputy coroner got out and came to the door firing questions at them. "What was William wearing when you last saw him?" Before he could ask many questions, the neighbor figured it out and said, "Wait a minute. They don't know yet." William's funeral was March 2, 1966. This was an immensely stressful and sorrowful time for my parents. It is only natural for a father to put his hopes in his son, yet my father did not become bitter at the death of my brother. He went on giving his best and living for others, teaching other young men how to chip arrowheads and build houses.

The year that my brother died, my best friend was killed in an airplane crash. I missed so many classes, that I failed one. My dad, instead of getting upset with me, calmly said, "I only ask that you apply yourself and do your best."

For my parents, suddenly life was just the two of them. My dad told me he missed the noise of kids in their home. Life changed for him again when I got married, and he gained a son-in-law and later two grandchildren. From the time my children were little, he encouraged them to go to college and told them he would pay for it because he had money saved for William's college education that he never used.

A friend of mine later wrote, "When I was in the fourth grade, more years ago than I normally admit to, the Methvin family moved into a house across the street from us. I spent so much time at their house that Ruth started calling me their dark-haired daughter. They became my tall parents. My adopted father, Ray, was a rock. He knew right from wrong, and he lived it every day of his life. Ray was part of the foundation Edna and Lennie built their family on. His legacy is part of the foundation that Scott and Shelley [his grandchildren] will build their lives on.

"There was never an angry rumor about Ray and some gal up the street. Ruth never had to administer, 'rolling-pin-therapy' because he came home inebriated in the wee hours. It just never happened. He loved his children, and he loved his wife. He was proud of Ruth. He cherished her."

Dad had a warmth about him and a love for people. He related to others by bending his tall frame down to their level instead of towering over them. His eyes sparkled as he talked.

It has been said that the image we have of God can be influenced by the image we have of our fathers. I have always been open to God because of the attributes I saw in my father. My dad was never preoccupied or unavailable. He was usually home when he wasn't working. He always gave me his full attention. There was no grunting "uh huh" from behind the paper. He was never only half-listening with eyes glued to the TV. He did not interrupt. He was a listener not a lecturer. He was always there for me, no matter how tired he was. He gave me security as a woman that so many women spend their lives seeking. My dad taught me how to live life, and he set the example. He gave me a strong sense of honesty and morality. He didn't teach me one standard and live by another. He never promised me something without doing it. He taught me persistence to stick to a job, do it right, and see it to completion. I never lacked his emotional, moral, and financial support, like he had lacked with his own parents. He could have treated his children the way his parents treated him, but he didn't. He was the dad everybody wanted.

WHO IS THIS MAN?

Dangerous?
A threat to others?
Uncontrollable?
Unmanageable?
A problem?

The bulletin board we hung above Dad's bed in each care facility

Through photographs and captions, the bulletin board we hung in each facility told the story of my dad's life. Here's a sampling of the wording from the captions: Ray Methvin: WW II airplane mechanic, logger, gardener, a man deserted by his father and yet a wonderful father to his own children. A man with honesty and character who taught by example. A man who denied himself luxuries to put his grandkids through college. A man whose neighbor's dog adopted him.

Each time Dad was settled in a new facility, his behavior showed him to the door. He was written off as a troublemaker. He soon wore a lot of labels. Though not visible, they stuck: "unmanageable," "uncontrollable," "a threat to others," "dangerous." All these words, like stepping stones, led in only one direction, to the door and "don't come back!"

I could handle those labels, they were just words, but I couldn't accept him being treated with lack of respect. One particular incident comes to mind. A former neighbor of Dad's, who was employed in a care facility, told me he witnessed the incident. My dad had messed his pants because he was not able to find the bathroom in time. The aide on duty said, "Come here you dirty old man, so I can change you." Dad tried to fight her while she was attempting to change him. She came out of his bedroom with a bump on her head. The neighbor told me, "I have known your dad all my life. He was well respected in the community and an artist," and he pointed to Dad's arrowheads displayed in a frame on the wall. "He should have the dignity he deserves."

Unlike that aide, I had the advantage of knowing my father all my life, and I wanted others to know him for who he was, not who he had become. I wanted them to know him as an individual, to know about his interests and accomplishments.

Because we lived in a rural area with only one board-and-care home and one long-term care facility, every time Dad was evicted, he was moved farther and farther away from home. The adjustment would begin all over again as he experienced a new environment, a new room, new caregivers, and new rules. No one caring for him knew the Ray he had been. As he continued to deteriorate, he changed from the gentle giant we loved to someone we barely recognized, not only in personality but in appearance. I shredded pictures of him from that time because I didn't want to remember him looking so bad. I also wanted people to know that the Alzheimer's and the psychotropic drugs prescribed to control him had turned him into the crazed person they saw.

It was important to me that anyone who was caring for him would see him as he was before, as a person not a problem. So I pieced together a collage of pictures of him as a son, husband, and father.

The bulletin board collage displayed the different facets of my dad's life. Now nurses and aides could appreciate who he was inside, instead of only seeing the wild-eyed monster who could keep the entire place in an uproar day and night. As he frustrated caregivers and frightened fellow residents, I wanted them to look beyond his behavior and the Alzheimer's that gripped his mind to the person he once was.

SCHOOL DAYS

Ray at grammar school (top left)

Ray at high school graduation
(top row, 2nd from right)

Ray in high school basketball team (top row, 3rd from right)

FAMILY

Ray (center) with mother Sally
and brother Romaine

Ray and his mother Sally

Left to right:
Electa (sister),
Ray, Cametrice (sister),
and Rondel (brother)

Left to right: Reuel (brother), Rondel (brother),
Colonel William Thompson (maternal grandfather),
Ray, and Romaine (brother)

DATING DAYS

Left to right: Ray, Ruth (future wife), Helen (Ruth's sister),
Chet (Helen's husband), and unknown friend

Ray's Master Mechanic certificate

RAY'S FATHER'S SECOND FAMILY

Ray with his father and his father's second family

Ray and his half sister, Lillian

RAY'S MILITARY DAYS

The Queen Mary, Ray's transport across the Atlantic during WW II

Ray as soldier in England during WW II

Ruth, 1944

Ray (right) with army buddy

Ray as an airplane mechanic

WESTWOOD, CALIFORNIA

Early days as a logger

The move from Massachusetts to
California after the war

Ray and daughter Edna May in
front of apartment in Westwood,
California

PONDOSA

Town of Pondosa

Methvin family at their home in Pondosa

Snow to the rooftops in the 1950s

Ray and Edna May

Ray working for McCloud
Lumber Company

McARTHUR

Methvin family, Ruth and Ray with children William and Edna

Methvin family in front of home in McArthur

Ray fishing with Edna and William

MARRIAGE

Early marriage

Anniversary party, 1993

FAMILY

Edna and Ray

Ray and Lennie, Edna's husband

GRANDCHILDREN

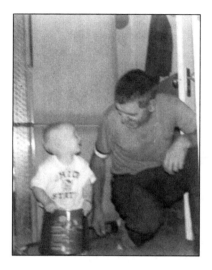

Scott and Ray

Ray and Shelley

Ray with Shelley and Scott

RETIREMENT

Ray helping build Lennie and
Edna's home

Ray in his yard

Ray demonstrating his hobby of
making arrowheads

A Life Within Alzheimer's

The best way out is always through.

—Robert Frost

In 1991 subtle changes, sneaking in unnoticed, began to occur. They went unnoticed for many reasons. Some appeared normal and were attributed to my dad's age. After all, in your eighties it's okay to be a little forgetful. If he forgot a name or didn't remember a person, it was perfectly acceptable because even younger people did that.

Dad always had a one-track mind. His habit of interjecting one more thought in a conversation that had long ago changed to another subject was typical for him. He had a habit of returning to the previous conversation as if the topic had never changed. So if he said something that didn't quit fit in, it was just my dad's way.

We didn't pick up on my dad's Alzheimer's because we attributed a lot of wrong answers to his increasing deafness. We expected him to give the wrong answer. If he didn't comprehend something, we figured he had just not heard correctly. He had worked around noisy airplane engines and power saws for many years before earplugs were required. So as wrong answers became more frequent, we thought he hadn't heard correctly. For example, once when he was staying with us, I asked him if he would like to ride out to the woods where Lennie was working. His answer was, "Oh, save the watermelon for the kids."

His hearing aids magnified sound in crowds and hurt his ears, so he turned them down. It became harder and harder for him to track conversations. His hearing difficulty lessened his involvement and interaction with friends.

Conversations with Dad became work. "What?" "Huh?" "What did you say?" My mother had taken him for many appointments at the hearing aid center. A new type of hearing aid was connected to a hand-held amplifier. Dad commented, "It works so good you don't dare fart!" But instead of handing the speaker to the person speaking, my mother became his interpreter and repeated whatever was said to him. Eventually each new type of hearing aid lost its effectiveness. My mother was the more talkative one and tended to answer for him, which made him more and more dependent on her. When Dad couldn't hear me, he looked to Mother to tell him what I had said. "Edna May wants to know if you are tired." He'd look at her and ask, "Who's coming tomorrow?"

He was left out of conversations because he didn't comprehend what was repeated to him. Once we got his attention and he responded, the first thing he would say was, "Speak up. How do you expect me to hear if you whisper?" So we would try again, and he would stop us in mid-sentence with, "Don't shout. I'm not deaf you know." Finally the attempt at conversation would end in frustration from both parties. When I asked a patient at the clinic why he didn't talk as much as he used to he told me, "You have to have a grasp on the conversation or you interject something and get laughed at. If you get laughed at enough, you withdraw." Because Dad became frustrated at social gatherings it was easier for him to stay home and let Mother go out alone.

I thought some of the problem was the way we communicated with Dad. I noticed he became increasingly confused if we switched subjects too fast. We tried to write notes, but he didn't think that was necessary. He thought the problem was the way we spoke to him—not his hearing. He never attempted to read lips. We learned to give him time to process what we had said. We tried to speak in simple sentences instead of paragraphs. Despite our efforts, wrong answers became more frequent, but we still wondered, had he just not heard correctly? In spite of regular appointments at the hearing aid center nothing was successful on a long-term basis. Nothing made up for all those years of deafening engines and power saws.

Dad tuned us out. Because he couldn't hear, he tended to withdraw into a world of his own, deep in his own thoughts, instead of making the effort to track the conversation. His world became smaller, and he dwelt more and more on the past as his mind withdrew to what had been familiar to him.

When Dad was eighty-one, we went camping with relatives near Lassen Park. We were sitting around the campfire listening to Lennie's Aunt Pearl, a former army drill sergeant, who always spoke with a booming voice that got everyone's attention. Dad sat staring straight ahead. When Pearl asked him a question, he did not hear until someone touched his knee and pointed to her. He said, "What?" and we realized he had no idea a conversation was going on as he sat looking at the campfire deep in his own thoughts.

As he withdrew, Dad had less input from the outside world. He was never much of a television watcher, so when his hearing decreased, he lost interest in TV. He was never into hunting. His camping days had come to a close. As he replayed his life in his mind, he got stuck in different time periods. He told his war stories to whoever came by. "Did I ever tell you about the time I was working on a Spit Fire plane on the airbase in England during World War II?" We listened attentively at first until he started repeating some of the same stories over again, and then we learned to just nod at the appropriate times and pretend we hadn't heard it before.

One day a friend who heard his stories for the first time told us, "Your dad is afraid he will get drafted to the Gulf War, and I know he's too old." By then something about the often-repeated war stories caught my husband Lennie's attention, too. Dad's war stories had changed. "Did I tell you about the time I was working on a Spit Fire plane on an airbase during the Viet Nam War?" Lennie had been in Viet Nam, and of course he knew Dad had served in World War II.

My mother depended on Dad for physical strength, and at first he was strong, even though he was failing mentally. They made a good team. He hauled wheelbarrows of gravel from the back yard to the driveway in front, and she instructed him where to spread it. He shoveled snow from in front of the carport and piled it where she showed him. In the summer he carried in arm-loads of produce, and in the winter, wood from the woodshed, and stacked it where she wanted it on the porch.

My mother depended on him to help her cross the street if traffic was heavy or if she had to hurry or if the roads were snowy or icy. She grabbed his arm so she wouldn't fall. Inside the house, she washed dishes and he dried. She showed him where to put the dishes in the cupboard. After he carried in groceries from the trunk of the car, she showed him where they went. He was willing to help, but he needed to be told what to do. She gave him directions for everything. He needed directions repeated over and over again. My mother laid out my dad's clothes from the day they were married, and always gave him directions, so taking directions was not new. It was a perfect combination, almost as if she was the mind and he was the body instead of two separate people. She was the instructor, and he carried it out. The problem was it became a habit; he did not have to think things through on his own. He became totally dependent on her.

One day, Dad and I were sitting outside on the lawn chairs, and I turned to him. I looked into his eyes. He was gazing off into the distance. I asked, "What are you thinking?" He replied, "I don't have to think, your mother does my thinking for me."

The changes started in 1991. My mother started hiring a handyman to do upkeep around the house that Dad would normally do. Her reasoning was that no eighty-year-old should be up on a ladder. She was afraid he would fall off the roof. While the handyman was there, it was easy for her to give him a list of other things that needed to be done. As a consequence, Dad had less and less responsibility and fewer problems to solve. His world became smaller and he declined mentally. He went outside less and less.

My parents had purchased the lot next door with the idea of tearing down the dilapidated building that sat on it to increase the size of their yard. Over the years the building had been a thriving restaurant, a shoe store, and an insurance company. Dad planned on removing the nails and re-using the boards. He wanted to get started on it, but my mother would not allow it. Because it was old and in poor repair, she didn't want Dad to be the one to tear it down. She was afraid that he might get hurt in the process. She said it was too great an undertaking for a man his age to attempt.

Instead of having a project that would keep his mind occupied and physical activity that would keep his blood circulating, he stagnated. So the building just sat there while my dad sat in his recliner. Would having something to do have kept his mind active and healthy longer? I will always wonder if tearing down that old building would have delayed the onset of Alzheimer's in Dad. Yes, he might have fallen off a ladder while repairing the roof. He may have fractured an arm of a leg or suffered a physical injury while tearing down the old building, but it would have healed. How can you repair a fractured mind? How do you repair the mind from stagnation and inactivity? We can't live life over, but I will always wonder what would have happened if he could have remained physically active and not had someone do his thinking for him. I wonder if the mental change in Dad was because he had no problems to solve and didn't have to think things out.

I'm aware of an opposite approach. A friend of mine has a father-in-law who is starting to fail mentally. When she was at her in-law's home, she went out in the yard and tried to help him do something he was struggling with. Her mother-in-law said, "No, let him be. He needs to figure it out himself. If it takes all day, it's okay. It's good for him to have to use his mind to think things through."

Most of us have difficulty remembering the day of the week when we are on vacation. It is easier to lose track of our days off than when we have work or appointments to keep or meetings to attend. Most of us have some reason to know the day, month, and year, and those reasons keep us engaged.

Even people in jail can be mentally engaged, even if it's with plans of escape. A man incarcerated in solitary confinement in Alcatraz told how he replayed in his mind every ball game he had ever seen to pass the time. He made his mind work. He maintained his sanity. A prisoner of war said that he kept himself from going crazy by making his world bigger. He passed time by playing all the songs he had ever heard on an imaginary piano. He made his world bigger than his circumstances, and he remained sane.

Dad's world became smaller as he limited the amount of input to his brain. His world required less alertness, and he ventured out less. He became more and more confined to the walls of his home and eventually confined to the walls of his mind. Instead of stretching, he stagnated mentally.

By contrast, my father-in-law suffered from a devastating stroke in his sixties. He was unable to speak clearly, had some one-sided deficits, and had to have someone dress him. Yet he fully recovered and lived a normal life. I believe he overcame his disability because each day he had a reason to get out of bed. Each day he planned a project and worked at it until it was completed. It helped him become stronger both physically and mentally. When he died at the age of eighty-three, he just got shorter and shorter of breath until he stopped breathing. His body gave out physically before he gave out mentally.

The greatest deterrent for Alzheimer's is to use our brain everyday. An elderly person said to me, "Honey, I'm almost ninety, but I can learn something new everyday." He was motivated, and he taught himself to set up and use a computer when he was ninety-five. Everyone can become forgetful or absent minded during times of stress. Here's a classic example: A friend's daughter was going into labor, and as her family was rushing around to take her to the hospital, the mother-to-be picked up the cat and put him in the refrigerator instead of outside. Luckily someone noticed. Anyone can have times like that; it doesn't mean you are getting Alzheimer's. Delayed recall is normal as people age. Alzheimer's involves progressive memory loss. Research into Alzheimer's now shows that mental stimulation can delay the onset and severity of Alzheimer's. I know an older woman who keeps a record of "Today I learned . . ." to challenge herself by stretching mentally instead of stagnating.

Many people fear they are getting Alzheimer's as they get older because they forget names and misplace things more frequently. According to Dr. Susan Kemper, psychology professor at the University of Kansas, "The problem is not if you lose your keys; it's if you forget what keys are for."

Dad had always been able to outwork most men and bragged that he looked younger than his age, so it was hard for him to accept that he was getting weaker and older. One day, when I stopped by my parent's home, Dad was outside mowing the front and back lawns with the push mower that he had always used. I said, "Don't you think it's about time you bought a power mower?" He replied, "I bought this lawn mower at the end of World War II for only ten dollars, and it's all I need." He continued with a smile and a twinkle in his eye, "Besides, it is run by power, mine." I didn't want to disappoint him by pointing out that at eighty-three years old, his power wasn't what it used to be, so I took the handle of the lawnmower, and he willingly stood by and supervised while I used my power.

One day I realized that I was standing eyeball to eyeball to Dad. Standing over six feet tall, he had always towered over me, and now as he became more stooped, he was almost bent to my height of five-foot-seven. Even though he still maintained his ideal weight of 185 pounds, subtle changes were occurring. His hair was now more white than gray. He didn't have the energy that he previously had. He spent more time dozing off in his chair and less time interacting. He had become disinterested in what was going on around him. Mother wrote in her notes, "Walks slow. Can't be hurried."

We noted other gradual changes. The arthritis in his hands was a physical loss. But it also meant a loss of his creative outlet and artistic purpose. He became less active. In winter Dad spent more time relaxing in his recliner in between stoking up the fire, and in summer, he didn't jump up every half hour or so to change the hose on his garden or flowers. One day when my mother was in Canada, and he was staying at our house, he was helping me take down Virginia creeper vines before I painted. He took a break, laid on the couch for a nap, and said, "You know your dad isn't as young as he used to be." In spite of the changes in his vitality, when anyone asked how he was feeling his reply was always the same, "If I felt any better, I couldn't stand it. My health is as good as ever."

As an RN, I know how grief affects the immune system. Our resistance is lowered after the death of a loved one. In addition to the loss of his siblings during the1990s, Dad experienced other personal losses. For example, he outlived a best friend and neighbor, Bill Burgess, with whom he had spent many hours discussing politics and engaging in stories while they were out in their yards. Loss and grief can take a profound toll.

In war-ravaged countries, it's documented that women have gone blind, with no physical or medical cause, because they lived through and saw too much tragedy and horror. That seems similar to the way Alzheimer's somehow allows its victims to subconsciously live in a protected place in the past where their primary loved ones are still part of their lives, instead of living in a world without them. They revert to a place in their mind where they don't have to face the reality of the present. Alcoholics and addicts have told me that it is too hard to wake up sober, so they drink themselves into oblivion or shoot up again because they can't face life as it is. The hurt is too deep. Maybe life is too hard when you experience too many losses. Maybe Alzheimer's victims live somewhere out there in a place protected from losses that are too hard to accept.

In her late nineties, a neighbor from Pondosa told me, "My world is passing me by. There's no way I can understand all the new technology. I don't belong here." I wonder if she didn't mentally return to a more comfortable time and place instead of living alone in a world that was rapidly becoming more foreign as her dementia increased.

Sometimes a realization of loss changes a person's mental awareness. Lennie's Aunt Beulah was very independent and outlived three husbands, but she rapidly lost ground mentally when she was doing the records for the Golden Umbrella, a senior citizen's organization where she had been a volunteer for many years. As part of the job, she documented the dates of births and deaths of all the friends she had outlived. Although she'd been very independent and capable until that time, she rapidly declined mentally and became unable to function alone after working on that project.

Some older people can't articulate their thoughts and feelings about growing old; others can. When I visited Ouida, a close family friend in her nineties, it struck me how candid she was about old age. She had never married and had no children. She was one of those people who became better looking with age. Somehow it suited her. We sat in rocking chairs on the porch of the cozy board-and-care home where she lived. As we rocked back and forth, she was very clear, alert, and talkative. She told me that at times she sensed her faculties diminishing. "Sometimes I feel that I am a shadow of my former self." I watched her small curved frame rock slowly back and forth as she spoke, and I listened to the creaking of the rocker. She stopped rocking and looked directly at me whenever she wanted to make a point, "I have been thinking about how all my relatives worked on oil wells and how the company towns were all painted the same color." She started rocking again, and told me how lonesome she was and how she missed having a home to go to, and she wondered why no one would tell her whether or not they had sold her car, because she didn't know what had happened to it. Then she stopped, pointed her index finger at me and said, "You won't understand now, but someday you will when the older generation is gone, and you feel so alone. You will miss them like I miss my Aunt Harriet and Uncle Guy [who raised her]. You need close family and friends." As long as Ouida focused on the oil wells in the company town, she was not alone in an unfamiliar world. I remember that day so vividly. Just after that she declined mentally and finally physically, and then she was gone.

In the fall of 1993, I noticed Dad was no longer driving. I asked him why. He said, "Oh, I made the mistake of dozing off at the wheel when your mother was in the car, so that was the end of my driving career."

My mother protected us by concealing the changes in Dad from the rest of the family, while he became more and more dependent on her. He had a hard time locating things, and easy tasks became difficult for him. As time went on, he needed more instruction and direction. If Mother was out of his sight, he constantly hunted for her. She was his only security and his buffer to the world. He started shadowing her. Mother wrote in her notebook, "He clings to me all the time." Dad's confusion increased to the pivotal day of the urgent and distraught phone call from my mother asking for my help.

By the time my mother called me for help in October of 1994, the familiar had become foreign to my dad. He looked to Mother for answers, "What do I wear?" "Who lives here?" "Who owns that?" "How many will eat here?" "Where do they sleep?" "Where do I sleep?" "Where does this belong?" "Where are my red shoes?" "Where are my glasses?" "I've lost my keys. Where are my keys?" When mother answered he would say, "Show me; you go. I'll follow."

We had spent years rationalizing and blaming his poor hearing for his unusual behavior and change in his demeanor, but by the day my mother broke down and called for help, even my dad recognized the change in himself: " . . . I think I am going crazy. There is something wrong with me, and no one has come to help me."

That's when I said, "Would you be willing to go to the hospital and see a doctor who is a friend of mine?" And he jumped up, and eagerly followed me to the car. "Finally someone has come to help me! I'm getting crazy in the head, you know." Mother had dropped her pretense of normalcy, and Dad was aware enough to know he needed help. Our family odyssey with Alzheimer's had begun. The trip to the local hospital was the first leg of that journey.

After spending the night in the hospital, Dad was confused until he looked out the window and said, "Why, there's Mt Shasta. Now I know where I am." Since his labs were all in the normal range, and there were no physical problems to keep him hospitalized, he was discharged to go home.

The immediate crisis was over, but because Alzheimer's had been lurking around in our family for a long time, we looked to the future with uncertainty and apprehension. We were face to face with the probability of Alzheimer's because all other causes for Dad's strange behavior had been ruled out with the lab work. It appeared that my invincible dad had survived a difficult childhood and the hazards of World War II but could not escape his family's legacy of Alzheimer's.

My mother knew that this was a turning point in our lives, and she asked my husband, Lennie, to accompany her to a lawyer to see that all their affairs were in order. She removed my dad's name from all important documents and replaced his name with mine. She also talked with Lennie about the kitchen remodel she had been planning. She got a bid from a contractor and arranged to have it done as soon as possible before my dad became more confused.

As Dad's Alzheimer's progressed that winter, she called Lennie for help again. She asked him to remove Dad's gun from the house. She also asked him to remove the wood stove and help her pick out a Monitor heater to replace it. She explained why. She had awakened with a start in the wee hours of the morning sensing that something was wrong, dangerously wrong. She smelled smoke and heard the crackling of a roaring fire. She ran into the family room to find my dad standing in the glow of the open fireplace door, stuffing yet another piece of wood into an already overstuffed stove. Building up the fire had always been his job, but now he no longer knew when to stop. He still had the physical ability to get the wood in and continued his usual chores, but he was unable to think things through. Mother managed to get the stove door shut but worried about what would have happened if she hadn't awakened when she did. Getting rid of the stove was the only way she could protect Dad from burning himself or setting the house on fire.

Because my mother could no longer hide my dad's behavior, her cover-up had to end. She seemed relieved that she no longer had to hide Dad's illness "to keep from worrying us." It was a weight lifted off her shoulders to be able to talk about what was happening instead of trying to protect us from it. She had previously layered her hurts deep within her, only allowing them to surface long enough for her voice to crack with emotion. Her eyes would brim with tears, as she held back the feelings that bubbled to the surface. She had not shared her deepest feelings with even her sister, best friend, or daughter. Keeping things to herself was a life-long habit, " . . . because no one wants anyone to feel sorry for them," she'd say.

Mother's emotional distancing started when her parents died. She was left alone at a young age. She buried herself in work and earned her way through college. Instead of focusing on the aloneness she felt, she chose to put her mind instead on the design in the material she was sewing or the petals and colors of the flowers she was arranging in a vase. She stayed very active, "to keep my mind off my problems." So it came as no surprise to anyone that she kept Dad's failings tucked neatly inside until the day came that she had to call for help.

Dad's anger and confusion had increased prior to when he was admitted to the hospital for testing, and my mother had taken him to their family physician to try to find a cause for his flare-ups. The doctor wrote in Dad's chart, "Is he losing it?" All tests were negative, and their family physician could find no contributing cause for his behavior. He prescribed Tegretol and told my mother it would help with the anger. My mother would give him one after every outburst. When that didn't help, she asked for something else, and the doctor prescribed Haldol, which she also gave him to help control his anger. Much to her embarrassment, before long she noticed an obvious wet spot in the front of his pants—the side effect of confusion caused by the medication. He had not been incontinent before. We realized that must have been a sad and embarrassing, but also frustrating time for my mother who was very private about any problem.

My daughter, Shelley, once wrote about her grandmother, "Always her things were in order. Her jelly jars and canned fruit were dated and labeled. Grandpa was one of the things she'd always kept in order. She'd lay out his trousers along with one of the shirts she had sewn to fit his broad shoulders. Grandma would always give Grandpa a once-over at the door before they left the house, more often than not handing him a comb for his thick gray hair or pointing down at his untied shoelace. It was these details though that brought Grandma a great deal of pride."

Despite the medication, his frequent bouts of anger continued. He became increasingly upset and irrational, and my mother took him to another physician for a second opinion. This doctor found all labs to be within normal limits, and as a quick screening test, she asked Dad to draw the face of a clock. He drew all the numbers and both hands on one side only, signed his name in cursive below it, and held it up proudly for the doctor to see, just as if his clock drawing was exactly as it should be. Again, every test was done to rule out everything except Alzheimer's.

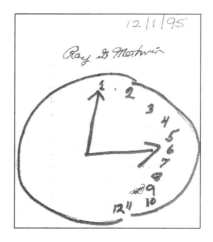

My mother's notes reflected Dad's escalating anger. "Ray got screaming mad at me two times in three days." I think he acted out because he couldn't describe what was bothering him. It reminded me of a boy who came in the clinic for a junior high physical and told me about an incident that happened when he was four years old. He said he had something in his ear, and when the nurse started lavaging his ears to get it out, he thought his brains were coming out, so he screamed and cried and fought the staff.

When my mother started sharing the reality of my dad's condition, one of the first episodes she told us about had happened the summer before. She had been feeling a little house-bound, so she packed a suitcase and drove Dad to Circus Circus in Reno for a weekend mini-vacation. She awoke at two in the morning to find that Dad was not in the room. She called security, and they located him downstairs wandering among the slot machines in his pajamas.

The confusing jig saw puzzle of Alzheimer's started fitting together. As the puzzle pieces fit, we began to see the picture clearly. Now my kids understood why my mother had rushed them off when they stopped by for their usual lengthy visit with their grandparents on their way back to college. They had left their grandparents' house hurt and puzzled when their grandmother met them at the door with her usual tins of home-baked cookies and said, "Here, I'll carry these things to the car for you and you can be on your way." They called to tell us about it later and said, "We didn't even get to say goodbye to Grandpa." More pieces of the puzzle came together from what friends told us. Betty, a neighbor from Pondosa whom my parents met each year for a little vacation on the coast, told us that in 1992, two years before we acknowledged Dad's Alzheimer's, that she had to show Dad how to play the card game "Spite and Malice," a game he had played for years.

We didn't pick up on Dad's Alzheimer's sooner for multiple reasons. As a nurse, I fell into the pattern of not being objective with my own family. Like a teenager who thinks he is indestructible and untouchable, because we'd always believed Dad was so healthy both mentally and physically, we were in denial. Like the typical family, Lennie and I were preoccupied with what was going on in our own lives: pursuing careers, attending college classes, earning degrees, keeping up with the schedule at work, and maintaining a home. We were also involved with Lennie's parents who lived next door to us and were in and out of intensive care during that time. We had kids in college, and Lennie was running a ranch as well as logging full time. Life was so hectic that the owners of the local pizza parlor told us that we were their best customers. I had no time to go to the store or cook. Like most people, we took for granted that my parents would always be there. I let other things crowd out the time I would have spent with them.

The other reason we didn't realize what was happening with my dad was that whatever my mother didn't cover up for, my dad did. I was with him once at a party when someone asked him the elevation of McArthur. Because he couldn't remember that it was 3,200 feet he said, "Oh, its 6,000 feet, but it goes all the way down to sea level." He was creative in his cover-ups. One day we were in a mall sitting on a bench waiting for Mother. I asked him if he knew what day it was. Of course he didn't, but he was pretty clever at improvising. He leaned over to a younger lady sitting near him and said, "Excuse me, we are trying to figure out what day it is. Could you be so kind as to help us out?"

As the Alzheimer's progressed, his interaction with others declined. He talked less and less and then responded only when someone reached out to him. The conversations soon became one sided. His presence and personality withdrew. Gradually he developed "that look," which is as diagnostic to physicians as "droopy eyes" is to a mother whose child is ill. He had that vacant, detached, unresponsive, "lights on but nobody's home" gaze. The spontaneity was gone. The twinkle in his eyes was replaced with gazing off into the horizon, looking straight ahead while walking past people as if they weren't there.

My mother had trouble with her hip prosthesis, and she depended on Dad to help her cross the street in traffic. He was able to hold her arm and keep her from slipping on ice, but he could not hold up his end of the conversation. Their chats over coffee and meals became one-sided. He talked less and responded less. For years my mother had done the majority of the talking, with Dad listening attentively, and commenting appropriately. Now the conversations that usually followed radio shows like "Paul Harvey" and "Unshackled" just didn't happen anymore. For my mother, communication and support was gone. She learned that she might as well be talking to the wall, and she missed Dad's presence in their life. But she wanted to be there for him and had no intention of his living anywhere but with her.

There are milestones in awareness and acceptance of my dad's condition. I remember a day I had off work in the spring when I'd made plans to start rototilling my garden. I wanted to get an early start on planting. My father-in-law, Arlo, told me the ground was too wet to rototill. I had the rototiller in place and was ready to start it. Arlo continued, "If you can form a ball of soil with your hand, it's still too damp. Ask your dad if you don't believe me." I looked over at Dad who was standing in my yard, not participating in our conversation at all. Oh, how I wished I could ask him. There were so many things about gardening and life, I would have asked him had I known I wouldn't have another chance. Things that I never imagined I would need to know because he had always been there to do it for me. Now Dad was there physically but not mentally, even though he was standing right next to me. I could reach out and touch him, but I couldn't touch what was keeping him from responding. I missed Dad, a strange thing to say when he was still alive. The irony of Alzheimer's is that they are there physically, but their mind is somewhere else.

Dad became more confused. On his eighty-fourth birthday, my in-laws and Lennie and I were at my parents' house for dinner and birthday cake. I brought a bunch of helium "Happy Birthday" balloons, but Dad didn't seem to notice. He was occupied with passing the placemat around with his birthday cards, "Here, take a look at this one too." On the way home my father-in-law asked if Alzheimer's was contagious. We assured him that it wasn't, and Lennie explained, "It's a case of the body outlasting the mind."

In the four years that Mother cared for my father at home, from 1992 to 1996, many of his actions and reactions were alarming and disturbing at the time, but in retrospect would be considered typical "normal" behavior for a man functioning the best he could with Alzheimer's. At times he reacted with paranoia and defensiveness to events that were very real to him, but in reality existed only in his imagination. At times his responses gave us a glimpse into how his brain was working, and sometimes his responses and reactions were baffling.

When my mother was leaving to spend four days in Sacramento with her sister, I had misgivings when I went to pick up Dad. I felt that he would do better in his own surroundings and planned to mention that to my mother, but when I pulled up in front of their house, there he was, suitcase in hand waiting for me. Even though we only lived a half-hour away, the drive thoroughly confused him. When my niece came over with her two children to say hello, he thought everyone lived with us in the same house. I showed him the bed I'd made up downstairs for him. I laid his suitcase, pajamas and slippers on it, so he would feel at home. Then he asked, "Where do I sleep?"

"This is where you sleep."

"Oh. Thanks for telling me."

As soon as we went in the kitchen to get something to eat he asked, "Where do I sleep?" We went back downstairs, and I explained everything all over again. When I was finished he asked, "Where do I sleep?" As soon as I explained again, he asked, "Where do I sleep?"

"This will be your bed."

"Oh that's a nice bed. Thank you," then, "Where do I sleep?" "Oh, that's where I sleep?" All as if he had not just asked and heard the answer moments before.

As he got ready for bed that night he asked, "Where will I put my hearing aides?" I gave him a container for them and put them on a shelf. Then two minutes later, "Where are my hearing aides?" "Oh thank you for showing me," followed by, "Where are my hearing aides?" Just when I thought we had solved the problems of, "Where do I sleep?" and "Where are my hearing aides?" he started with, "Where is Ruth?"

I found that after answering him several times, it was much more effective to write it down: "Ruth at Helen's." I referred him to the note each time he made a path to my bed during the night to ask where she was. The note seemed to satisfy him more. He would doze off for a couple hours, shuffle to the bathroom, loudly raise the toilet seat and then make a path to my bed to ask where Ruth was. Finally I said, "It is good for her to have some time at her sister's."

He replied, "Good for Ruth but not good for Ray."

The next day he was able to pile branches and rake leaves and seemed almost like my old dad again. That four days with Dad clarified for me what day-to-day life was becoming for my mother. For the forty years they lived in McArthur, part of my parents' daily routine was to make a trip to get meat from the chest freezer they kept in the thick-walled pump house twenty yards from the house. Mother also kept her home-canned jars of fruit, jam, and tomato sauce on the shelves. After Dad got whatever Mother requested for dinner out of the freezer, he'd locked the pump house with a padlock before he returned to the house. Now he needed Mother to show him how to find the freezer. This time she went ahead of him, and while she had her back to him reaching for one of her frozen pies, she heard the thick door close as Dad went outside. Then she heard him clumsily attempting to padlock the door. He had forgotten she was still inside. The pump house was so well insulated, no one would have heard her cries for help, and there was no window for escape. Dad would have forgotten where she was, and she would have been trapped inside. Mother managed to get Dad's attention and push the door open before he pushed the lock in place. A catastrophe was averted.

Dad had a lifetime habit of sitting in his recliner in the living room reading the paper and letting sections fall to the carpet as he finished reading each section. When Mother was there, she kept the papers picked up, but if she was away from home, when he was finished, the papers were spread out in sections in a semi-circle around his chair. As his Alzheimer's progressed, he continued the same routine, only without comprehension of what he read. He'd read the paper straight across, because he included the advertisements as part of the articles. What he read did not make sense to him, but he still read. Later he would read the paper over and over without turning the page. He could not comprehend the meaning of the words. His ability to read didn't change, but his ability to comprehend was gone. Once as I was passing by his chair, I noticed a headline in the newspaper he was "reading." It read: "Orwig enters a no-contest plea." He looked up at me and said, "I thought I saw an earwig." I showed him the headlines and asked him if it was because of "Orwig." He said yes. That day he had his bathrobe on over his clothes because he was cold, which was unusual for him. He looked at me and pointed to one sleeve of his bathrobe and said, "This one is shorter than the one the newspaper is sponsoring."

There was a loose connection in his brain like an electrical wire that flickered on and off depending on how it made contact. One time in his yard, he looked up at the apple trees and said to me, "They sure need to be pruned but what the hell, I'm retired, I'll do it next year." As we walked back to the house, past the garage, he looked in the open window at his lumber pile. "I sure do have a lot of lumber in there, don't I?" Then he added, "I didn't get the lumber pruned in there either, did I? It sure needs it."

Sometimes a word would be linked to another word with a different meaning. Once when he was leaving our house he missed a step in the entry way, and he fell and rolled, " . . . like I learned in football." He was unhurt but "falling" made him think of his years in the woods falling timber, and he began talking of his days as a logger. It made me wonder how his brain synapses worked. It was as if a link that tied one thought to another was often circumvented, but sometimes the synapses short-circuited and connected thoughts that shouldn't have been connected at all.

During a Thanksgiving as he was eating a bite of turkey, he heard a coyote howl outside and asked if coyotes ate turkey. Instead of his brain working as a whole unit, it was like a string of Christmas tree lights going out one at a time in his brain, and not getting replaced, leaving blank unlit spots. On Father's Day, I took a present to Dad. As I handed him the gift-wrapped box he asked, "What's this for?" When I told him it was his Father's Day present, he looked at me with a puzzled look on his face and said, "Oh, am I a father? Nobody told me."

The frequent outbursts of anger started in 1994. Attempting to reason with him only compounded the problem. His anger was all out of proportion to what was happening. Ouida, a close family friend who practically lived with my parents, said to me one day, "Your dad has been screaming mad at your mother over the smallest things. He really has been flying off the handle a lot lately." Unusual behavior became more and more commonplace.

Dad's mood swings were challenging to deal with. When our daughter, Shelley, saw that her grandmother needed a respite day, she took her to lunch in Mt. Shasta, and I stayed with Dad. He was angry. "You can go too. I don't need to be babysat." He was so angry that he threatened to turn his hearing aids down if I talked. Any attempt at conversation was met with a glare or a snarl. But in a few minutes, a good aspect of forgetfulness kicked in, and he forgot he was mad. He forgot he didn't want to talk. He told me, "I'm touched in the head." I tried to politely disagree with him in an attempt to make him feel better, and he said, "Well, no matter what you think, that's how I feel."

Sometimes he forgot; sometimes he remembered events that had never happened. A neighbor, Johnny, who had grown up next door to my parents and still lived nearby, called me. "I think you should know that your dad confronted me in the alley at the gate to my berry patch and threatened to kill me. He blamed my dad and me for stealing his pipe dies. He said we borrowed them twenty years ago and never returned them. I've never seen Ray so mad in all my life. He took a swing at me but stumbled and missed and fell down. Your mother came out and escorted him home." After my mother marched Dad home she called Lennie.

"Ray," Lennie said, "you returned the pipe dies to Reuel, that's why you can't find them." Dad never owned any pipe dies, he had borrowed them from his brother Reuel and returned them to Reuel.

Dad acknowledged that Lennie was right. "Thank you, Lennie, for straightening me out. I guess I didn't know the difference between what was real and what I was dreaming. I guess I was hallucinating." He reached out to Lennie and shook his hand. Lennie drove home feeling good that he had helped resolve the neighborhood problems.

The next day Dad decided that Lennie was in a conspiracy with the neighbors to not only steal his tools but his house too. A man who had lived peacefully alongside his neighbors for half a century was now threatening to kill them for stealing "thousands of dollars worth of tools." The more he fixated on it the bigger it became. Not long after that, my parents were walking at the fairgrounds, and someone overheard Dad shouting at my mother, "I just want peace."

Sometimes we couldn't get him to let go of his anger and obsession over something that he imagined. An apple tree that belonged to my parents' neighbors dropped apples on both sides of the fence. One day when Dad and I were at the restaurant across the street eating lunch, Dad was glaring out the window, looking back across the street. He didn't eat, and I couldn't divert his attention. He said, "I sprayed Hiram's apples for years, and this is the thanks I get. Now he is purposely letting them drop in my yard." He saw the falling apples as a plot to infect his apples with worms. Nothing could convince him otherwise.

Dad had lived next to the bar for almost fifty years, and it was a common occurrence for cars to park in front of his house as they pulled into the bar next door. They occasionally blocked his driveway. Now, he became increasingly upset and out of control if a car even partially blocked his driveway and would stand with a scowl on his face as he looked out his living room window, guarding his driveway from those who plotted to block it. Paranoia and anger are common with Alzheimer's patients, and they can't be reasoned out of their obsessions. They may forget about it sooner or later, but reason and common sense won't deter them.

Clearly, Dad's condition affected not only our family, but others as well. One day as the noon whistle sounded, the whole town became aware of the changes in my dad. He confronted his eighty-four-year-old neighbor on Main Street. The people gathered for lunch at the local restaurant saw Dad walk out to the yellow line in the middle of the highway and challenge his neighbor Hiram to a fistfight. A crowd gathered. Someone told me later that they were placing bets on which one of the "old codgers" would win. Dad had obsessed on the notion that Hiram was purposely letting his apples fall on Dad's side of the fence in a plot to infect his red delicious apples with worms. Now Dad was ready to have it out with Hiram and settle the issue once and for all. He walked toward Hiram for a show down like in the old western movies, but instead of a gun he had his fists raised. Hiram was saved from going down for the count. Dad had difficulty making a fist because of the arthritis in his hands. No one won the bet that day because both sides bet on the wrong person. Onto the scene came my frail seventy-eight-year-old mother. Physically, she was no match for either of them, but size didn't matter. She was mad enough and embarrassed enough to walk into the fight and bodily drag my 185-pound father off the street and into a cold shower "to cool him down" as she threatened him with divorce.

He screamed at her for an hour, saying that the Crums had stolen a thousand dollars' worth of tools and had a big parade. When he calmed down, he agreed there were no new tools and no parade. After the incident was over Dad said to Mother, "I can't go on like this. Isn't there an institution you can put me in?" Dad told me later that one of Hiram's brothers threatened him if he tried to hurt Hiram again. Dad's response was, "That's okay, I can whip the whole bunch of you."

We noticed that his disruptive behavior seemed to go in cycles. He would be fine for about three months and then be disruptive and unmanageable. For years Dad and his neighbor, Hiram had shared a brown dog—just a mutt—named Bruno. It was an agreement that worked for Hiram, Dad, and Bruno. Bruno had adopted Dad and never left his side except when Hiram came once a day with a leash to take him with him to the post office to get the mail. Hiram always put Bruno on a leash, or the dog wouldn't leave Dad's side. Dad couldn't object because after all, Bruno was Hiram's dog, too. Their shared ownership had been acceptable before, but now Dad dwelt on it and found it unacceptable. The more he dwelt on it, the madder he became at Hiram, even though Bruno always returned as soon as Hiram let him off the leash. My dad's anger at Hiram for walking Bruno became an obsession. But as time went on and Dad's world became smaller, he forgot all about Bruno and never even noticed that Bruno was gone and never inquired about him. The pound picked Bruno up, and when Hiram's wife got him back, she put him in a makeshift pen. Bruno tried to jump the fence and in the process hung himself. Dad had been as devoted to Bruno as Bruno was to him, but Dad had simply forgotten him.

In March of 1995, a patient at the medical center where I worked commented, "I'm almost as crazy as your dad." She explained that she and her husband were pouring cement to make changes to their porch next door to my parents' house. "Your dad came over and just lit into us. Left us shaking our heads wondering what brought that on. So out of character for him," she said, still shaking her head in bewilderment.

Dad deteriorated in this order: First he became disoriented in time. It often appeared that the present was mixed in with a time frame of events and people from his past. Next, he became disoriented to place; once-familiar places became foreign to him. Not reliably recognizing his family and people he knew soon followed. Then he lost the ability to recognize the difference between male or female. And finally he lost the ability to recognize himself.

He not only lost the day and month but also the year and the time frame he was living in. My daughter Shelley was going to West Virginia to do a photography internship, and my parents were at our house for dinner when she was discussing her plans. Dad said, "Be sure and look up Dad when you are there. He was nice to me, and he will be nice to you also." He didn't comprehend that his father had died in 1964 before Shelley was even born. A friend my age who I grew up with was visiting Dad. She asked him if he knew her. He answered, "Of course, I'd know you anywhere. You're Paulette." Then he ruined it with, "I haven't seen you since the war, have I?"

He became disoriented on roads in the same valley where he had lived for years. After a very familiar drive to our house, he asked what state he was in. When we answered he said, "Thanks. I'm relieved to know I am in California. I really didn't know." He got lost between towns, then between the alley and the highway on each side of their home where he and my mother had lived in since 1956. Next he got lost between the back and front yards. One day my mother found him wandering around the yard with a wheelbarrow full of crushed rock, unable to find the place to dump it. Then the day came that he could no longer find his garden. Then he got lost between the kitchen and the family room at either end of the house. Ultimately he could get lost between the bedroom and the bathroom. The area in which he'd lose his bearings went from many miles to just a few feet.

Dad's recognition of us, his close family, became less and less reliable. He had always known my mother until one day he looked at her and said, "I like you because you make up your mind quick, just like Ruth does." Once when I went to visit, I had a friend from work with me. When I introduced her to Dad, he said, "Pleased to meet you." When I looked at him, I realized he was looking at me. Sometimes his level of recognition depended on the setting or circumstances: Dad had been visiting at our house, recognizing and responding to Lennie and me. Lennie drove Dad home from our house. Dad later told my mother, "I am so thankful for that nice young man who brought me home." He didn't recognize his son-in-law of thirty years nor realize it was Lennie driving him home, although he had just known Lennie in the familiar setting of our home. Being in the car, a new setting, changed Dad's degree of recognition.

March of 1995 was a real wake up call for all of us. My daughter stayed overnight at her grandparent's home so that Mother could visit her sister. Shelley wanted her grandfather to feel independent and less like he was being "babysat" while Mother was away. When they went out for lunch, she let him pay for the meal. But she regretted it because he became convinced that the waitress had intentionally given him the incorrect change, and he spent all afternoon checking and rechecking his wallet, like the six-year-old boy who had come to our home selling soccer candy bars. The boy looked up at his mom because he couldn't understand that the five-dollar bill and coins I handed him was the same amount as the dollar bills he expected.

The next morning Shelley was making coffee when Dad entered in his pajamas. He shocked her when he said, "What's your name? I don't know you" She replied, "Shelley." "Sally? Oh, pleased to meet you. That was my mother's name also." She still couldn't believe he didn't know his only granddaughter. She had grown up near him and had seen him at least once a week. "Grandpa, you know me. I'm your granddaughter Shelley!" But he didn't. Then he said, "I'm sorry to ask your name. You know I'm slipping."

Dad would go months at a time without recognizing me. I could tell immediately when he knew me. "Look who's here, it's my daughter, Edna May." It was not as hard on me as it was on the grown son of an Alzheimer's patient who went to visit his mother on Mothers Day. As he was leaving he bent down and gave her a kiss on the cheek. She slapped him because she did not recognize him.

Not recognizing family members is common with Alzheimer's patients. A friend of ours took care of his father until he died. One day his father asked, "Who are you?"

"I'm your son Randy"

"How long have you been my son?"

"Forty-three years."

"Oh, I'm glad you told me, I didn't know." Then they drove downtown to a hardware store, and his dad recognized a man he had worked with a few years before and called him by name.

Another friend received a call from her father in the middle of the night, "Please come and tell your mother that I am her husband. Even though we have been married for fifty years, she wants me out of here. She's saying, 'What will the neighbors think? A stranger living in my house?'" When she arrived her mother was saying, "Who is this man?" What is he doing here?" When she was admitted later that week to long-term care, she introduced the new young male aide as her boyfriend.

In May of 1996, just before Dad was admitted to the first care facility, Mother and I attended a mother-daughter luncheon and fashion show at the fairgrounds a block from their house. Lennie stayed with Dad and took him across the highway to the local restaurant. When the luncheon was over and Mother and I arrived at "Wild Bills," we found Dad and Lennie sitting in a booth. They were finishing their hamburgers, fries, and coffee. Dad looked at us and said, "Hi! Lennie was here, but he left a little while ago." It wasn't Lennie who left. It was Dad's mind. How could he not see that Lennie was still sitting at the same table with him? Especially when he had recognized Lennie that day and called him by name. It boggled my mind. I realized then Dad was losing more ground daily, that he was not "holding his own." How could my mother continue to care for him?

Inability to recognize gender is not uncommon with Alzheimer's patients. One day my dad said to my mother, "You are Romaine."

She told him, "I am Ruth."

He replied, "But Ruth is a female."

The husband of one of my patients said to me, "Do I look like a momma? That's what my wife just called me."

Inability to recognize themselves is also rather common and disturbing to all concerned. I heard about a man who told his wife there was an old man living upstairs, and he pointed to the mirror. A woman I took care of as a home-health nurse would look in her mirror and scream. She didn't recognize her own image. My dad too, did not always recognize his own reflection or picture. And with my dad, the day came when he didn't recognize his own body parts, and he said, "I can't find my penis."

In February of 1996, after Dad's brother Rondel died, Dad became more and more confused. But one day in April, the window to his soul opened, and he had a lucid moment. He looked at Mother and asked, "How long have I been this way?" My mother realized she could not continue the twenty-four-hour care with no respite. Dad's overnight hospitalization was the first reprieve she had had.

My parents lived on a state highway in the middle of a town that cars sped through because there was nothing to slow down for and no reason to stop. We realized we could not allow him to remain at home so close to a potential accident. We knew something had to change when I received a call from some close friends. "We think you ought to know that we were driving through McArthur in the middle of the day and saw your dad crossing the highway without looking for cars." That same night I received a call from two nurses who worked the night shift at the hospital. "We were on our way to work and saw your dad wandering on the highway in the dark." That did it. I couldn't handle the idea of Dad getting run over by a car. I grew up on that highway, and we learned to judge the speed of the cars as they whizzed through town before we crossed to the store on the other side. Dad no longer had that judgment.

Highway 299 East is the main street of McArthur, making the town a small, wide spot in the road. I had lost many pets while I was growing up because they tried to run across the highway in front of cars. The two girls who lived across the street lost many pets also. We picked up their flattened, mashed bodies and put them in a shoebox and carried them to the alley behind our house. We dug a hole in the dirt and buried them. And then we had a little funeral service for each pet and placed a cross on top of the grave. Near the fence in the back alley you could see the little white crosses with the names painted in childhood writing: Blackie, Teddy, Misti, Snookems, Freddy . . . . I didn't want that same fate for my Dad. I told a neighbor, "I can handle anything except Dad getting run over by a car." She said, "There are some things worse than death you know." I couldn't think of anything worse.

By then my mother was exhausted from the twenty-four-hour care. She only left him alone for an occasional appointment. I decided the best thing I could do for my mother for Mother's Day would be to place Dad in the local board-and-care home scheduled to open that month. I had no idea that my making the decision my mother was unable to make would be the beginning of a complete role reversal between my mother and me. Our roles of the complacent daughter and take-charge mother reversed, to Mother turning every decision regarding Dad over to me. I think she was relieved that she no longer had that responsibility.

My mother was reluctant to move Dad out of their home, but she agreed to a trial basis. I insisted it was necessary. She could no longer leave him home alone because he didn't have the judgment to look for cars or the ability to dial 911 in case of fire. Then my mother received a call that her sister Helen's daughter had died of breast cancer. She wanted to be with her sister and comfort her. I convinced Mother to put Dad in the new local rest home, Riverbend. To eliminate her resistance to taking him out of his own home, I told her that the move could be temporary while she was at the funeral, just to see how Dad did in the rest home.

* * *

Dad became the first resident of Riverbend in May 1996. Riverbend was located in a nice looking one-story, five-bedroom home on a hill in a nearby town. The living room was spacious with comfortable furniture and large windows overlooking the river. Mother packed only enough clothes for Dad for a one-week stay because she wanted to make sure he would do all right before making the arrangement permanent.

After we arrived, Dad willingly followed us up the ramp to the front door. Even though we had explained what we were doing, he was oblivious to what was going on. He was warmly greeted and welcomed with a handshake by Riley, the new owner. Dad responded positively to the attention and followed Riley indoors.

Mother started putting away his things in his small bedroom. She put his razor, toothbrush, and comb on a shelf in the bathroom that was directly across the hall. Dad, Riley, and I sat at the big table in the dining room, and I started filling out the required paperwork. When Riley asked Dad a question, he replied, "You'll have to excuse me, I don't think as clearly as I used to, and I don't want to play possum and pretend I do. There's something wrong with 'it' you know," and he pointed to his head.

Somewhere in the process of filling out the paperwork, Dad thought he was being discharged from the Army. He leaned over and shook his thick head of hair for us to examine and said, "Whew. That almost gave me a gray hair or two. Do you see any?" He still saw his hair as dark brown even though it had started turning gray decades earlier and was now totally white.

As soon as the paperwork was completed, Mother took him to his room and showed him where his things were. When she was done, he asked, "Where's my razor?" She took him across the hall and showed him his razor, toothbrush, and comb. "Oh, now I see. Thank you for showing me." But as soon as he returned to the living room, he asked again, "Where's my razor?" She showed him again. He paced back and forth asking the same question repeatedly. He finally quit only long enough to ask, "Where's my comb?"

When it was time for us to leave, Dad said goodbye to us. Then Riley engaged him in conversation so that our leaving wouldn't be a problem. When Lennie came after work to see him, Dad told Riley, "Lennie's here now to pick me up, so I'm leaving." Lennie handled it by saying, "I think you're supposed to stay for dinner, Ray." After dinner he had forgotten he was leaving.

A dark haired, middle aged, good-looking woman worked the night shift that night. When it was time for bed, she came into Dad's room and helped him get ready by unbuttoning his shirt. As she started to undo his pants, she was interrupted by the phone ringing, so she left the room to answer it. As she was talking on the phone, she heard loud scraping and shuffling noises. When she got back to Dad's room, she discovered the door was barred, and she was unable to open it. She asked Dad to open it, but he wouldn't. The shuffling noised continued, so she ran outside to look in the window and see what was going on. Dad had barricaded the door with the bed, dresser, and nightstand.

She ran back inside and shouted through the closed door, "Ray, what are you doing?" He replied, "You're not going to sleep in this bed with me!" She didn't understand his reasoning or his actions, but to those of us who did, it made perfect sense in the time frame he was reliving. Dad was in a strange place with yet another woman trying to get a soldier into bed. Alzheimer's may have taken a lot from him, but it didn't take his morals. He had retained his high standards in spite of all the women in foreign countries making passes at him. He saw the caregiver as just one more young woman trying to take advantage of a soldier. She was puzzled, but we understood all to well. He was reliving his army days.

The next night Riley decided it might be better if he stayed instead of the female caregiver. Dad was up wandering around at midnight. Instead of reasoning with him and telling him that it was the middle of the night and he should be sleeping, Riley said, "Ray, how about having a bowl of Cheerios with me?" So they both ate Cheerios and milk at midnight. After they laughed and had a good time talking, Dad was content to settle down and sleep.

The following night, Riley was not so lucky. He relaxed on the couch after getting Dad to bed, hoping to catch up on the sleep he had missed the previous night. Riley's long, lanky legs and cowboy boots hung over the end of the couch. He put his cowboy hat on top of his western belt buckle, crossed his arms and fell into a sound sleep. At two a.m. he was awakened suddenly by Dad standing over him shouting, "What are you doing in my house?" Dad shook

Riley's arms, demanding an explanation. When Riley opened his eyes, he could see from the anger on Dad's face that he was in trouble. He knew it looked to Dad like he had just discovered an intruder sleeping in his house. It took some quick thinking on Riley's part, but he was able to convince Dad that he was not an intruder. "I'm a friend of your daughter, Edna May, and she invited me to stay." Riley was perceptive enough to know that his attempts to convince Dad that he owned the facility, or had a right to be there, would be fruitless. Instead, his answer seemed to pacify Dad, and he relaxed his grip on him.

For a while, Dad was the only resident of Riverbend. Even at that, he was a challenge. Sometimes he was pleasant and easy to care for. At other times he was confused and disruptive. The owners learned by doing and made adjustments accordingly. They discovered that Dad could not find the bathroom, because when he walked out of his room, he had three directions to go, and he was incapable of making a decision. They moved him to a room with a bathroom, and he did much better. There was a direct route to the toilet, and he had less incontinence. They discovered that when they had their grandchildren over after school, there was too much noise and confusion for him, even though he loved kids. They noticed patterns to Dad's behavior and moods. He became stirred up and restless with too much stimulation if the TV was on and the children were running around. He became agitated because he couldn't process all the activity.

Each day was a new day for Dad as he adjusted to his surroundings. After being confused in the home he had lived in for fifty years, he now had to adjust to a totally new environment. During the adjustment phase, there were multiple opportunities for situations to either escalate or be diffused. Just before Halloween, Dad pointed to the bowl of candy on the table and asked, "Who's trying to poison me with all this candy?" Thinking he was joking, we commented, "No one," and went right on talking about something else. That was not an acceptable answer for him, so he became more insistent. He felt someone was trying to poison him, and he wanted to know who it was. Riley finally pointed to me and said, "She is." He laughed. I laughed. Dad picking up on our mood, laughed too, and that was the end of it.

Soon another man was admitted. He became good company for Dad, an audience for his war stories. The man spoke loud enough that Dad could hear. Dad didn't realize that the other resident's stories didn't make sense. He enjoyed his company and was interested to hear someone talk about the old days.

Dad enjoyed being outside. But the Riverbend owners found it necessary to fence the yard when he started wandering down the road. They allowed us to bring his push lawn mower over even though they thought someone might criticize them by claiming they made a resident do the work. Mowing the lawn gave Dad purpose, responsibility, and independence and made him feel useful again. He went from being very confused and unsure of his surroundings to imagining that he built all of Riverbend. Sometimes he would rake leaves, and we were all happy to see him content and occupied. When I asked him how he was doing he said, "Oh, I couldn't be better." When he was inside, he enjoyed working on large jigsaw puzzles.

Dad continued to get his words mixed up. A woman resident moved in. She was having a telephone installed. He told me, "She's getting a phone because you know how women like to cab." I knew he meant "gab" because he moved his thumb and middle fingers back and forth like a mouth opening and closing. The woman had a small dog with her, and the dog occupied Dad and made more company for him.

Dad had been very dependent on my mother and asked frequently, "Where is Ruth?" The caregivers always replied, "Oh she'll be here later. She's gone shopping again." When she visited, and it was time for her to go home, they would distract him by showing him the arrowheads he made years before. Their techniques worked for diffusing potential problems.

Sometimes Riley would drive the men to Burney, twenty miles away, for haircuts. Then he would take them out for a hamburger and fries for lunch. Since Dad was the only resident at first, he received a great deal of attention and interaction, which helped him to adjust and feel that he belonged. It was a wonderful transition from home.

As Dad settled into his environment, we felt comfortable that we could take him for an outing. One day as we were returning him to Riverbend, he looked up and saw Riley on the porch and said, "There's Romaine." We discovered that Dad, like a director of a play, "cast" people into different parts. I knew immediately what years of his life he was reliving by what name he called me as I entered the door. If he said, "Here's my sister, Electa," I knew it was before she died. If he said, "Which bus do I take to Cametrice's house?" I knew it was when he was in Los Angeles going to aeronautics school. I learned to listen closely to find what time frame he was in. I could figure it out if he gave me enough clues.

One time I found him in the back yard at Riverbend raking leaves. He stopped, looked up at me and said, "Mother's dead isn't she?"

I assured him that she wasn't. I said, "No. She was just here a few minutes ago." I could tell from the look on his face that he didn't believe me.

"You ask someone else, and they'll tell you that I am right," I said confidently. He leaned on his rake and one by one listed each brother and sister by name. "Is Cametrice alive?"

I answered, "No."

"Is Rondel dead?"

I replied, "Yes."

He said, "Well he's better off." Then he said, "What about Electa?" I told him that she had died. Then he asked about Reuel and Romaine, and I had to be honest and tell him that they were gone also. "What about Mother?" Then I realized that he had been asking about his mother, not my mother. No wonder he was confused. I had confused him all the more by talking about my mother. Then he finished with, "What about Ray?" Then he laughed and said, "Well, Ray might not be dead, but he's slipping."

I wish I could have been there in the August of 1996 when Dad had a window of clarity that lasted almost half an hour. Riley said it had been an ordinary day. Suddenly Dad looked at him and said, "I need to go home. My wife will think I left her." Riley asked him where he lived and he said, "In McArthur with Ruth. Down the road about four miles. Whatever did I do to get myself in this mess? How long have I been this way?"

Sometimes I was there when the brief moments of clarity happened. They were glimpses that allowed him to look outward and us to look in at the person we knew was locked inside. Like a window shade briefly pulled up, so we could see inside his soul before the shade was pulled down again. One day we were outside on the patio when Dad looked at me expectantly, "Where did these coins come from?" When I shook my head and shrugged my shoulders, he became upset and demanded an answer as he rattled the coins in his pocket. "Who put these in here?" Then to my amazement, he had a brief moment of clarity that lasted only long enough for him to reach over, touch my hand and say, "I want you to know that I love you." As quickly as the moment came, it was gone, and he returned to rattling the coins in his pocket and repeating, "Who put these in here? Where did these come from?" Moments like that were unexpected gifts. No one knew what caused them to surface. He would leave me feeling robbed when he disappeared again. These moments of clarity continued to happen even when we thought he was in the later stages of Alzheimer's.

Mother would sometimes call and tell us she had been to visit Dad, and he didn't know who she was. If Dad recognized Mother he would say, "Oh, there's my sweetheart." One time he mistook me for Mother and gave me a kiss on the cheek as I left. My mother said his eyes would sparkle when he recognized her. It was as if he was the one wondering where she had been. There were rare times when Mother knew he was aware as she hugged and kissed him, "He was so happy to see me. He cheerfully gave me a hug and a kiss." Other times it hurt her to see his emotional absence and expressionless face or even worse, when he would think another female resident was his wife. When she left for a visit out of state for two weeks and called to ask "Does Ray miss me?" no one knew what to say. If they said that he didn't, she would feel bad. If they said that he missed her, she would feel guilty about being gone.

Visit after visit, we found ourselves making conversation more with the caregivers than with Dad because he was preoccupied or disinterested. Then just as we were accepting the fact that it apparently would be all down hill, he would surprise us.

Marvin was a very solidly built, short, stocky caregiver who probably weighed 250 pounds and was at least twenty years younger than Dad and at least a foot shorter. He had taken care of Dad for over a year and knew what to expect from him as well as anyone. Marvin was experienced and good at handling Dad. "If he fights me when I try to change him, I just do something else for a little while, like clean his glasses, and then he lets me. If he wanders out the gate, I just walk with him for a while, and then he tires and willingly follows me back."

One day Marvin and Dad were sitting in their recliners in the living room relaxing after dinner. Dad was thin and stooped and now weighed only about 150 pounds. After quietly sitting there a while, Dad looked up at Marvin and said, "Whose house is this anyway?"

Marvin, wanting Dad to feel at home, looked up momentarily from what he was reading and replied, "Yours Ray." Wrong answer. Something clicked in Dad's brain. He was out of his chair in a flash before Marvin even realized what was happening. He promptly bodily ushered Marvin to the front door, threw him out, and locked the door behind him. Marvin had to run around the house, sneak in the back door, and call Riley at home to come and intervene. In Dad's reasoning he probably thought, "If this is my house, this guy has hung around long enough."

The hardest part was never knowing what was going on in Dad's mind. In winter, on a rare day of good weather, Dad and I walked outside during a visit and sat at a table on the back patio. He repeatedly pulled his hand in and out of his pants pocket and asked over and over again, "Where's my pocket knife?"

After a while I got tired of it, so I tried distracting him by pointing to the roof and saying, "Look at the snow on the roof; that's more than we've had in years." He looked at me incredulously as if I were the one with Alzheimer's and said, "What's the matter with you? There's no pocket knife on that roof."

Dad's behavior problems seemed to run in cycles. Sometimes it was difficult to tell what would bring on a catastrophic reaction. It seemed to be anything out of the ordinary. One day he got upset because a glass of water had a lemon in it. Other times, something or someone may have triggered a memory from the past. One day a friend of Riley's came to the door. He had long hair and a beard. A chain of keys dangled from the belt loop on his Levi's. Dad wanted to fight him. We were concerned when we heard about it and asked Riley what happened. He said calmly, "Oh, he left," so apparently they derailed the fight before it happened.

The big problem was that when Dad got upset or difficult to handle, Riley would call the doctor, and the doctor would increase the dosage of his medication. It was a vicious cycle because the medication increased his confusion, and his confusion made him more difficult to care for. His compulsive behavior increased with the increased medication. He started getting up from the chair twelve to fifteen times each meal. He would put both his hands on the table and pull himself up, as if to see if he still could stand. Then he would fall back into his chair only to start the same routine again. It was like watching a robot programmed to repeat the same movement.

One day Dad was sitting in his recliner in the living room. They had allowed him to bring his favorite chair from home. He had his feet propped up. As he was lying back looking at the ceiling, he said to me, "I think I'll retire. They say I'm too old to work."

I asked, "How old are you?"

"Sixty."

How could he believe he was almost twenty-five years younger? How could he forget that he had retired twenty-two years ago? How could twenty years have just vanished from his memory?

He continued to ask about his brother Rondel. "He's in pretty bad shape, isn't he?" When Mother told him Rondel was no longer living, he would say, "Oh, no one told me." Each time he was told, it was as if he relived the loss, because to him, he was hearing it for the first time.

One day when we went to see Dad, he spent the whole time putting a foot in his shoe and then in his slipper. As he did, he leaned his chin on his hand with his elbow on his knee, with a puzzled look on his face as if he were in a shoe store and undecided about which of the two to buy. "Which one do you like best? Which one do I buy?" And finally, "Now, who do I pay for them?"

Another time he spent the whole evening getting into and out of bed. He would crawl into bed and pull the covers up around him and then get out of bed and put his feet on the floor. He repeated the same motion over and over again. He finally gave up, and got in bed saying, "I don't know if I am up, down, or sideways." Lennie thought he was probably getting up and down because he couldn't remember if he was getting into bed or out.

In December of 1996, Dad's condition had deteriorated to the point that he repeated one sentence over and over again, "I'm in a helluva fix." The next week, he had moved on to a new phrase, just as meaningless, "Egads, what now?" followed by, "I don't think we need to know Spanish, do you?" I would love to know how his mind worked and what brought a certain subject up or what triggered it to go on to a new repetitive loop. Another day, he would say over and over obsessively, "They take in the most money on Fridays." Such spells of repetition were particularly disturbing.

By 1997, one year after he was admitted to Riverbend, he was much more disoriented and uncertain. "What shall I do?" "Whose pants are these?" He was slower physically, and unsure of following even simple directions. Sometimes though he was aware, "I've lost some of what I had up there. I am fading. I have lost myself." When someone showed him a frame of arrowheads he'd made hanging on the wall at Riverbend, he said, "Who made these?" He didn't remember or recognize his own work, even though he had been making arrowheads since the age of eleven.

One night I had a very vivid dream that Dad died. It was so real that I woke up. I called out for Lennie and cried. I could not picture life without Dad. I knew I was being selfish. It made me realize that I was not ready to lose Dad no matter what shape he was in. So on New Year's Day 1997, I prayed and asked God to let me have him for one more year, "Then you can have him for all of eternity." I asked that I have him not as a zombie or vegetable and not bedridden in a nursing home. I prayed he would not deteriorate piece by piece. I asked that somehow he could gain back the ground that he had lost mentally. I prayed that there would be a change in Dad's behavior that was evident to everyone. I asked that the end of his days would get better instead of worse.

I bargained with God not only to let me have Dad for one more year, but that he would know me one more time. When I told my husband about my prayer he said, "You can't tell God what to do. You need to give your dad to God and leave the rest up to him." But I had prayed my prayer, and I didn't want to change it. I had seen too many answers to prayer in my life to doubt its power. I believe that God acts in the lives of men today, not just in Biblical times. I believe God designs things to happen as a result of our prayers.

I knew that I couldn't renew Dad's deteriorated brain cells. As I looked into his eyes, I wondered what was going on in there. How could he be declining right before our eyes? No one seemed to be able to manage him or control his behavior. I wanted him to gain back the ground he had lost. Most of all, I wanted some coherent time with him. He hadn't known me in five months. I realized that Alzheimer's makes you let go of someone when otherwise you never would. I couldn't accept losing Dad, but now it was becoming harder to see him have to live like this. I read, "The Lord looses the prisoners," (Psalms 146:7). He was a prisoner of his body and mind. I wanted him to live, but I wanted him to be in his right mind, or I wanted him to be set free. "Man's days are determined; you have decreed the number of his months," (Job 14:5). I knew, ultimately, how long Dad lived and in what condition was up to God, but I still asked for one more year. I believe God answers prayer; that's why I prayed.

Within the next month, as I entered the door at Riverbend, a coherent female resident greeted me, "Have you heard? He's back. Your Dad's back." She told me she had a normal conversation with him. When I entered Dad's room, he looked up at me and said, "Hi, Edna May." After a good visit with him, I had to leave for an appointment in Redding. He said, "You're going to Redding? I was hoping you could stay a while." I was hoping he could stay a while too.

I saw other answers to prayer at Riverbend. When he was on multiple medications and the side effects lowered his social inhibitions or when his Alzheimer's took a turn for the worse, he would stand in front of the ladies in the sunroom zipping and unzipping his pants, and no one could do anything about it. It was embarrassing for all of us. Once I saw him in the sunroom trying to undo his belt buckle. Dad would never have done anything like that in his right mind, and it made me understand more why the owners wanted him moved. That night I prayed, "Lord, please give him a new fixation. His mind seems to work like a record player stuck in a groove. Please move it on to something harmless." When I called two days later, the owner said, "Your dad has been really good lately; he spends all his time taking his shoes off and putting them on, all day long."

Life was more like a roller coaster than a downhill slide for Dad. Just when he seemed to be deteriorating the most, he would reappear when least expected. On his eighty-seventh birthday, he was much clearer than on his eighty-sixth. As Mother and I and some friends walked through the door at Riverbend carrying a cake and presents, he greeted us with a look of recognition in his eyes, "Hello!" It didn't seem to confuse him that there were extra people there for his party. He showed interest in an article on logging that someone had brought for him. The cook asked him what kind of pie he wanted and he said without hesitation, "I'll have banana cream please." He stood up to blow out the candles as we sang "Happy Birthday." After opening his presents, without prompting, he stood and made a speech. He looked at everyone around the table. "Thank you for the cards and presents. I appreciate them very much. I am thankful for my wife and for my family. I am grateful for good health. If I felt any better I wouldn't be able to stand it." The next day he was back to his previous patterns of behavior and communication.

Because I, not my mother, had signed Dad into the facility she discovered over a year later that the caregivers did not know that Dad had a partial plate in his mouth. Mother was there one day as they were brushing his teeth, and mentioned it. No one knew. They took him to the dentist office and sure enough, it was there, horribly caked in his mouth.

When we took Dad to our house for Christmas, he needed help opening his presents. My daughter-in-law hoped to make him feel a part of things, so when he wandered into the kitchen, she handed him an open box of croutons and asked him to put them in the salad. He got mad at her and stomped out of the kitchen, and he said over his shoulder, "I'm no cook." After dinner Dad headed into the kitchen to dry dishes, since that had always been his job at home. My niece was washing. She looked over at Dad. He had a dishtowel and was drying a stack of dishes. "Ray, those dishes haven't been washed yet."

He smiled and said, "I won't tell if you won't tell," and went right on drying.

People would ask me, "How can you go see your dad when he no longer knows you?" I always replied that I went to see how he was and to make sure he was being taken care of. If he knew me, that was an added bonus. If he had a few seconds of clarity that was even more rewarding because it happened so rarely. It made up for all the other times put together, and it made up for any miles I had traveled. It more than made up for all the days, weeks, and months of looking at a blank wall that no one could penetrate—the stare that looked through us but not at us.

People who take care of Alzheimer's patients know that what's going on in the patient's mind is very real to the patient, and it's likely something they had experienced or felt at some time in their life. Some say Alzheimer's patients live their lives in reverse, like a movie played backwards. From the experiences with Dad, it was like an old-fashioned reel of a movie of his life from 1910 to the 1990s put in a blender, shredded, and spliced back together. What he was experiencing in his long-term memory seemed to be a kaleidoscope of people, places, and experiences. It was similar to a weird dream—parts and pieces of scenes playing together. There may be some connection to reality, but a lot of their reality makes no sense at all. If only we could understand their movies it might give us a picture of how Alzheimer's patients see life.

Just as we "play life forward," looking ahead to the future, the very old reflect back. When we think of the multitude of experiences, situations, and people within a lifetime, and the capacity the brain has to store information, it is no wonder that no one understands exactly what causes a memory to surface or be buried. Experiences are normally recalled by the senses, and it is that very thing that makes it so hard to understand what an Alzheimer's patient may be reliving at the moment. We did learn that if we listened long enough, whatever movie was going on in Dad's mind became more clear to us.

Once when my son went to visit his grandfather, Dad thought Scott was his school chum from grammar school, Bill Smith. No amount of orienting could convince him, and it was easier for Scott to become Bill Smith. And that's what he did. In that same time period, the male aide caring for him became his brother, Romaine. Having those people in his life in the present was real to Dad, but to us there was just no way to connect the dots.

Dad's hearing deficit and Alzheimer's meant that most of the time, he didn't get the correct meaning of what was being said. He must have perceived his surroundings as if he was watching a movie on TV with the mute button on. He picked up on the feelings and moods and body language of those around him, because their words didn't have coherent meaning to him. If the ones caring for him became frustrated, tense, and uptight he picked up on that and added to their frustration with his own tense behavior.

When Dad became upset or difficult to handle and the doctor increased his medication, not only did the increased meds add to his confusion, his incontinence became worse. It was a vicious cycle because he would have more incontinent accidents, and then fight the caregivers when they tried to change him. He was on Tegretol to control anger, and he took the full course of Aricept for mild to moderate dementia. These medications didn't work for their intended purpose but instead did the opposite, worsening his symptoms.

The Aricept caused confusion and the anti-Alzheimer drug Cognex made him dizzy, confused, agitated, and unable to sleep. He was on Paxil, an antidepressant with side effects of nervousness, decreased appetite, anxiety, abnormal dreams, and again agitation. When he took Melatonin, an herbal product for insomnia, he became rude and combative. We described his behavior to the psychiatrist/internist and told him we attributed it to side effects of the medications. The drugs were discontinued, and there was noticeable improvement in his behavior until the next cycle, and then medications were increased again. It was a vicious downward-spiraling circle. He would be "pleasantly confused," calm and easy to care for, and then he would become upset—usually due to a disruption in his environment. He would act out and be difficult to care for. Alzheimer patients do better with consistent care in a consistent environment, regardless of any behavior cycles.

One morning he was so confused when he was getting dressed that he tried to put his under shorts on over his head. He was frustrated, angry, and swearing at the young woman who worked there who was trying to help him. Then suddenly he stopped and looked at her and said, "I'm no good and I shouldn't be here."

The hardest time for me while Dad was at Riverbend was a brief window of clarity, very similar to his window of clarity with Riley, when Dad seemed perfectly normal. He asked me, "Whatever did I do to get myself into this mess? I didn't do anything wrong. People are going to say that I left your mother. I want to go home." When I asked him where home was he answered correctly, "Right down the road in the next town."

By January 1997, the owners of Riverbend wanted Dad moved. Dad's behavior was worse, and the owner told us that he needed to be taken to Redding for testing. I was afraid it would be a one-way trip, like it was for another resident, who was taken to emergency and didn't return. I asked the owner, "Does this mean out the door?" He said, "No, but it will be if you refuse the testing." His premise was that maybe further testing would determine whether something else was responsible for Dad's behavior, and if not, then confirm that his behavior was due to the downward spiral of Alzheimer's.

The options for care were limited and expensive. My parents didn't qualify for Medi-Cal subsidies. Someone suggested to my mother that she divorce Dad, so he would qualify for Medi-Cal. She refused. Divorce was not an option; she had married him for better or worse.

After Dad was diagnosed with severe senile dementia, the owner of Riverbend said the only way he could continue to keep Dad was to move him to a smaller, older house they called the Annex. Among other things, Dad was peeing in the Riverbend sunroom in front of the ladies. Maybe the tree-like houseplants reminded him of his days as a logger. Because there were no bathrooms in the woods, any tree would do. Dad would never have done anything like that if he were in his right mind.

The owner of Riverbend also suspected Dad was touching "the girls." Dad had tried to get one of the female residents into the bedroom with him because he was convinced she was my mother. It made me understand all the more why the owners wanted Dad moved. When Dad started undressing in the sunroom, the owners made the decision to have only female residents. They were frustrated, and rightly so. I felt utterly helpless because I couldn't change the course of the disease or determine what would happen to him in the future.

I prayed that if Dad's mind was gone, God would speak to his spirit. I also prayed that he would be able to get off any medications that were making him worse. I asked that God would do from within what no human could do from without. I prayed that somehow he would gain back the ground he had lost mentally.

Dad had been at Riverbend for a year and a half. We moved him to the Annex in mid-August 1997, and he was the sole resident there. Because the owner had to hire separate help, the cost of his care increased. Dad continued to decline because there was no activity, nothing much going on, only a caregiver who listened to music or watched TV or talked on the phone. The owner hired younger, less experienced help who had no knowledge of Alzheimer's, and they didn't know my dad. For some it was a merely a babysitting job. Once again Dad had to adjust to new surroundings, and it was difficult for him. There was nothing for him to do. With no mental stimulation or activity, his confusion increased, and he spent more and more time in his room.

Dad's relocation to the Annex wasn't enough for the owner of Riverbend. Riley still wanted us to move Dad elsewhere. He even drove my mother to Redding to look at other facilities. Then Mother and I went together to look at them again on my day off. One was a complete maze of hallways and doorways that anyone in their right mind would have gotten turned around in. We liked a small facility in Burney, but they wanted only women residents and refused to take men. Dad was "private pay," and the cost for some facilities was prohibitive. Insurance would not pay for in-home care, and my parents didn't qualify for Medi-Cal.

My mother and Riley even contacted the Veterans Affairs Clinic in Martinez, five hours away, in their continuing efforts to find another facility. Everyone has something that touches them in the deepest part of their emotions. With me it was Dad. Maybe my mother could think of having him five hours away, but I couldn't. Maybe they could talk of moving him out of the area, but I couldn't.

Dad began to pick up on the fact that they were looking for another place for him. His comprehension level and his vocabulary were not what they used to be, but he was still able to recognize the attitudes and actions of those around him. It saddened me to hear him repeat, "I want to go home. Whatever did I do to get myself in such a mess? I'm no good. I shouldn't be here. How do I get out of this prison? Nobody wants me. They'd be crazy in the head to want me."

The Annex at Riverbend wasn't a good solution for his condition because no stimulation was as detrimental as over stimulation. Even as a nurse, I felt inadequate and didn't know what to do to help. I'd heard Dad say, "I'm in a hell of a fix." I wanted to fix the situation for him. All he ever wanted was a home. It was unthinkable to move him miles and miles from his home, and I wasn't even considering it.

I saw one other option. Quit my job, stay home, and take care of Dad myself. Several people cautioned me against it. The doctor I worked with told me that we can't think objectively with our own family, "No one can; that's why doctors don't care for their own families." And, he told me I was needed at work.

My husband pointed out that Dad could fall down the stairs of our two-story house. "Besides you may be able to quit work and go without sleep, but one of us has to earn a living," he said. "I have to leave for the woods at three in the morning, and it's too dangerous for a logger to try to function without sleep."

Probably the most effective argument against my taking care of dad came from Marvin, his caregiver at the Annex. Marvin was usually aloof and tuned into his classical music, but he sat me down and had a serious talk with me. He said, "I hear you are planning on taking your dad home and caring for him. You need to realize he is not the same dad you knew. You want to care for your dad? You have no idea what you are in for. Look, if you're so insistent on doing this, I'll tell you what, I'll make it easy for you. You come down here and stay with him for twenty-four hours and then see if you can do it. One girl quit the other day because he talked to her about intercourse and pooped in the middle of the floor. You have a good relationship with your dad, why ruin it by letting him pee on your walls and poop on your rug?"

But I was determined. If I couldn't care for him in our house then I wanted to have a mobile home set up on our property and hire caregivers for him. I couldn't move Dad far away without first trying to care for him at home. My mother had asked me, "What will happen to Ray if something happens to me?" I was glad that setting up a place on our property gave my mother the assurance that Dad would be taken care no matter what. As it turned out, the decision was taken out of my hands.

We had the approval for a second residence on our property, the septic tank was in place for a mobile home, and a caregiver lined out. I returned home from work one day and there was a message on our answering machine from my mother, "Lake Dwelling in Redding will accept Ray, so Riley's moving him to Redding today." At that point, it was not just Dad's living situation that needed resolving, but the angry feelings inside of me. I didn't want to move Dad out of the area without first being given the chance to care for him. My husband told me I was letting my emotions convince me that caring for Dad in our home would work when in reality it wouldn't. With Alzheimer's, you're not only dealing with the behavior of the stricken loved one, but your own feelings of hopelessness, helplessness, frustration, resentment, and lack of control.

Elizabeth Kubler Ross said in her book, *On Death and Dying,* that at times of loss, people go through specific stages of grief—denial, anger, bargaining, and depression—before they reach acceptance. Maybe I had skipped to the bargaining stage, not ready to give in, but with my dad's move to Redding, the anger stage caught up with me. I was mad that Alzheimer's was attacking Dad; mad that I had no way to defend him; and mad that I could only watch as events unfolded that took us deeper into helplessness. Even though everyone told me it would not work to care for Dad on my property, I was mad and frustrated that I was not given the opportunity to try. Life felt like one hurdle, one ordeal, after another. I wanted things to be easier. Why was this happening? I had no control. Looking back, I realize we never see a purpose in our problems until they've passed.

*   *   *

I have to admit that there were times I questioned God. In the Bible, David saw God's hand in everything. I struggled with seeing God's hand in our problems with Dad. I thought my way was the right way, and I "knew" I could make my way work. Then I remembered the verse, "You say the way of the Lord is not right? Is my way not right? Is it not your ways that are not right?" (Ezekiel 18:25). It was out of my hands, and I had to believe that there was a plan for Dad's future other than mine. I prayed that God would teach me to trust him when I didn't understand and that he would show us his solution.

On the trip to Lake Dwelling in Redding, about an hour and a half away, there were five of us in the car: Riley and his wife, my mother, Dad, and I. I sat in the back seat next to Dad. We all talked on the way down, and at one point Dad said, "Where are we going, Timbuktu?"

We passed through the big intersection near Burney where Highway 299 and Highway 44 intersect, and Dad said, "Oh, now I know where we are; there's the road to Westwood." He had lived in Westwood for only a year, but he recognized that road. He didn't recognize the road ahead of him that led over Hatchet Mountain, a place where he'd worked, and a road he'd traveled regularly for years. He didn't recognize the road to the right to Pondosa, where he had lived for nine years, and that was the same road to McCloud that he had traveled regularly for twenty years. What was going on in his brain that it blocked out everything except certain periods in his life?

Finally we arrived in Redding, and Dad looked at me and said "Well, hi!" as if he had been totally unaware that I had been in the car next to him for the last hour and a half.

When we entered Lake Dwelling, I thought, "How can this possibly work?" It was immaculate, like a setting out of *House Beautiful* magazine or the lobby of a high-class hotel, beautifully decorated with soft music playing in the background. Nothing about it even vaguely resembled a typical old folk's home. It looked like a resort, and at the same time, it was appealing to the pocket book, not as high priced as other facilities we had visited. Well-dressed, nicely behaved residents sat in tapestry chairs with matching pillows. Some residents were non-communicative but well behaved as they sat at the tables in their wheelchairs. There were beautiful dried flower arrangements and paintings on the wall. Mirrors added to the décor and made the facility look even bigger. I wondered how Dad could fit into this perfect setting. An imperfect person in a perfect setting, how could this ever work?

Enter Ray Methvin, who could disrupt everything. The resident sitting near the door said, "You better hurry or you'll get left." Dad didn't know that he really was getting left. We did the usual paper work, and the management asked us not to come back for a week, until Dad was adjusted and familiar with his new surroundings. We got Dad settled in and we left.

Whenever we called, a nurse or whoever took our call told us he was in the "adjustment phase." It was an adjustment phase for all concerned. Dad had no idea where he was or where his family was. He accused someone of taking his glasses and caused a scene. They turned the place upside down until they found where he had "hidden" them. Then things went from bad to worse when he thought my mother had run off with another man, "I'll never let her go without a fight." And he gave the man a black eye.

At first they were able to control him. We'd call, and they'd tell us, "No more problems. When he's agitated, we take him for a brisk walk." One problem behavior was that when he was tired, he'd attempt to take a nap on any bed he happened to find. That didn't sit well with the other residents who were used to having their own space.

His behavior entered a negative cycle. With Alzheimer's patients, we do not always know what triggers out-of-control behavior, it is usually a reaction to something that upset their usual routine that they can't process. They cannot handle physical and emotional stress. They can't tell you what's wrong with them or what they are feeling. Because they are overwhelmed and cannot communicate what is bothering them, they act out their frustration. Dad tried to walk out. When he was not successful in walking away, he tried scaling the fence. It didn't help that he was incontinent and fought the aides who tried to change him. He found a tall, tree-like houseplant to pee in when he couldn't locate a bathroom. He took off his clothes. So like the last facility, this facility asked for more medication to control his behavior. What was a temporary fix turned into a long-term nightmare when he started experiencing side effects and interactions of the medications on top of the behavior problems that came with Alzheimer's. Instead of the medications calming him, they had the opposite effect.

Dad's time at Lake Dwelling was a repetition of the previous scenario. Even though he was confused, he got along well at first. Then his confusion led to wandering, which led to an increase in prescriptions to help limit his misbehavior. One reason Dad reacted so badly to the drugs was because all of his life, no matter how sick he was, he would only take an aspirin. He had always believed in letting things run their course. A little medication went a long way with him. The medications lowered his social inhibitions and caused even more problems with his behavior. His confusion increased and the side effects caused him to be more defensive and harder to handle. For example, he didn't like it when someone approached him from behind and tried to direct him without first making eye contact with him. It startled him and made him defensive. The standard procedure with overly defensive patients was to request an increased dosage or a stronger medication. The cycle of increased medications and increased side effects spiraled. It was frustrating and even maddening, but we continued to do our best to be actively involved in his care and well-being.

When we took him to see his doctor, who was both a psychiatrist and internist, the doctor asked if Dad had been sleeping. Mother and I looked at each other and admitted we didn't know. The doctor, aware of Dad's hearing problem, leaned close to his ear and said very slowly, loudly, and deliberately, "Ray, how . . . have . . . you . . . been . . . sleeping?"

Since Dad was unable to think abstractly, he answered just as slowly and in the same tone, "On . . . my . . . right . . . side."

As we left the doctor's office, a boy, probably ten years old, was just coming in and held the door for us. Because Dad was stooped and the boy was small, their eyes met at the same level. "Well hi!" the boy said. For the first time someone approached Dad slowly on his level. The boy simply looked at him and gave him time to respond. The boy smiled at him and seemed fascinated to see an old bent man. Dad was happy to see a young person, since he'd been in a facility where there were none. They seemed equally intrigued with each other as they stared and smiled, and then the moment passed.

It was hard to know what to expect with my Dad. When my mother visited one day in October, he was doing great, talking with the other residents and in a good mood. My eighty-four-year-old mother and her ninety-year-old friend decided to take my dad for an outing in the park. It was a beautiful and warm fall day, but their enjoyment soon ended. They had the park to themselves, which was unfortunate because they needed someone to help them when Dad fell down. He was unsteady on his feet from being over medicated and could not get up. My mother and her friend tried, but because of his size, they were not able to lift him. They struggled and struggled. They tried pulling and pushing him, but nothing worked. My mother was just about to go find a phone and call for help when Dad finally managed to get himself up. The next day when they went back to visit, he had a black eye and did not know my mother at all.

Shortly after that, the aides caring for him noticed a change in his behavior and told me that they thought the medication was building up in his system. Aides are the first to notice changes when they take care of the same patients everyday. Aides see things first hand on a daily basis. They see subtle signs that aren't always noticed by a nurse passing out medications. They know what normal is, just like a mother knows when something is wrong with her child. I learned to ask the aides how he was doing, and they were the first to warn me that he was overmedicated. I would take that news as a red flag to be prepared for increased behavior problems. His pharmacy bill had gone up to several thousand dollars a month. My mother would soon be paying as much for his medication as for his care.

At Christmas I insisted my daughter visit Dad because she would be driving through Redding on her way home for the holidays. I thought everyone should see their grandparents at Christmas time. I realize now that it's a mistake to pressure family to visit, just because it's traditional to see each other on holidays. Shelley was unprepared for how much worse he looked since her last visit. She wanted to remember her Grandpa the way he was while she was growing up. Because I'd been seeing him on a regular basis, I didn't realize how bad he looked until I saw the photos from her visit. He was pale, wild-eyed, and over medicated. The pictures were so upsetting I tore them up. Shelley and I both regretted that she had seen him that way. As they sat next to each other on the couch, he gently reached over and poked her on the chest like a small child and asked, "Are you a boy or a girl?" "I'm a girl, Grandpa," she replied, to the same Grandpa she had known and loved all her life.

He started peeing in the corners at Lake Dwelling. Each time there was a crisis that almost sent him to a behavior center in Lodi, it was resolved. One time he hit another resident, and the staff wanted to "5150" him—have the police declare he was a danger to others and himself and be removed by police escort. Each time we passed a crisis, we got our hopes up that maybe this time it would work out for him to stay there . . . until the next incident happened.

By December he had picked up on the fact that he had worn out his welcome. We could tell because he kept repeating, "Nobody wants me." He said the words over and over again as we were sitting at the table with him at mealtime. There were four or five non-verbal elderly women sitting with us who appeared completely out of it except for one, who cussed constantly. I sat there with Dad, who said over and over, "Nobody wants me." After a half hour of "Nobody wants me," I couldn't handle it any more and said, "Of course they do. They love you." Then I heard "The hell they do!" I turned to the lady who cussed and it was not her. It was a twilight zone experience to realize that it was one of the zombie-like ladies who never spoke who said those vehement words. This otherwise silent lady continued to look me in the eye as she emphasized her statement, "They don't love us." She had not uttered a word in years. Something triggered a response, whether it was Dad's repetition or my insistence that they were loved.

My mother received a call on Christmas Eve that Dad had hit someone in the face. She hated to spoil Christmas, so she waited to tell us we had to move him again. I contacted the local doctor I worked with and said, "You say you always like a challenge. I have one for you. Would you be willing to take Dad as a patient?" He readily agreed. We drove down to Redding to get Dad and move him to the local hospital. When we arrived, at Lake Dwelling there was a staff person waiting at the front door with all of Dad's belongings packed in a black plastic bag. The minute we arrived she helped us load him in the car, so we could be on our way. They didn't want to keep him there a minute longer than they had to.

Before we left town, we ate at Burger King. Shelley and Tony, her future husband, met us there. This time Shelley and Dad had a great time together. She came to introduce him to her fiancé. But instead of confusing him by telling him she was getting married when she wasn't even sure he knew who she was, she entered his world. She waited for him to make a movement and then she would copy him. If he crossed his legs, she would cross hers. If he scratched his nose, she would scratch hers. Soon she had him laughing and responding to her because she was doing what he could understand instead of using language that only confused him. She told us, "I communicated with Grandpa with my eyes."

My husband decided to go through a car wash as we left Redding with Dad. As the brushes, colors, and sprays hit the car, I thought our quick in and out at the car wash must be what every day felt like for Dad—things coming at him in all directions, things he didn't know how to interpret or what to expect next. He would adjust to one onslaught and another would come at him. Dad sat motionless during the car wash. I couldn't help but think how peaceful and normal it must be at Lake Dwelling without Dad there.

As Dad continued his downhill spiral, the only thing we could count on was the belief that there was a solution we couldn't see. We knew the hospital close to home was temporary; the cost of long-term care there was prohibitive because it was double the cost of care at Lake Dwelling. We had no idea what to do, but we had to believe that somehow there was a plan and a purpose in all of this.

We headed away from Redding and back over Hatchet Mountain with Dad and his belongings except for one missing slipper. Dad was awake but said nothing. A new year was coming and a new beginning. We wondered what 1998 had in store for us. Maybe the next place would be better. When I told someone that I was praying for 1998, they responded with "Let the year come as it may." We were headed into a new year with a lot of unknowns. We had no idea what to do with Dad or who would care for him. With his stay in acute care at the local hospital only temporary, we knew we needed to find another long-term care solution, but we had no "plan B."

As I rode along in the back seat and looked at the scenery going by, and as we climbed back over the mountain, this scripture kept going through my mind, "That the Lord may show us the way we should take and the thing that we may do,"(Jeremiah 42:3).

*　　*　　*

At the end of December 1997, Dad was admitted to the local Valley View hospital for "exacerbation of Alzheimer's." He was placed in the only room available, directly across from the nurses' station so they could keep an eye on him. At least here at our local hospital, he was close to home.

Dad recognized us as we got him settled down and sitting on the bed. As we prepared to leave he said, "Let me know when you are ready to go. I'm ready to go whenever you are." How could we tell him we were going, but he had to stay, especially when he didn't feel bad physically? We were able to leave when he was distracted by dinner. He asked, "When will you be back to take me home?"

The doctor knew his history and sensed my concern. He said, "Don't worry, it will work. We'll make it work." I relaxed knowing my dad was in the best of hands.

Dad ate well while he was in Valley View hospital because he was under my mother's supervision. He smiled whenever she came in. He walked with her down the hall. Things seemed to be going so well that we considered admitting him to the long-term care unit in spite of the financial drain. It was so much easier for my mother to spend time with him near home instead of having to drive over mountain passes to visit him.

But without my mother around all the time, he was confused and disoriented. He could not find the bathroom, and was not used to being confined to a bed. He was in the same room as another Alzheimer's patient who was in a wheelchair. The man's arms and legs were in constant motion. He also had a tendency for violence and hollered constantly. When Dad first arrived he shook hands with the man, but the handshake turned into an arm wrestling match, prompting a call to the nurse.

There was noise from the overhead speaker twenty-four hours a day at the nurses' station, and to make it worse, it was the Christmas season with extra activity and people visiting. One of the concepts I was taught in the nursing program was the reality of sensory overload. A patient in an intensive care unit experiences beeps, lights, procedures, and interruptions twenty-four hours a day. It's like a casino with the constant noise and commotion. Sensory overload occurs when the senses are stimulated at a rate and intensity beyond what an Alzheimer's patient can handle. My dad was suffering from sensory overload.

Dad had lost the ability to understand what was occurring. He could not interpret the sensory input. Our senses—taste, smell, hearing, touch, and sight—are our trusted friends that help us survive in our environment. Without an ability to process what is happening, they become our enemies. We noticed a pattern with Dad. When the stimulation was reduced, he was much easier to handle. The more outside stimulation he had, the harder he was to control. He interpreted stimuli coming at him from all directions as something he needed to defend himself against. If he perceived the environment as friendly or frightening, he reacted accordingly.

Dad was already in an unfamiliar setting with a roommate in constant motion and distracting noise coming from the nurses' station. When he started wandering, people would come at him from behind trying to direct him. His hearing loss compounded the problem because he couldn't understand what people were saying. Dad did his usual wandering but could never find his room and usually ended up in the wrong room. Each hospital shift meant different people would be trying to direct him or keep him from wandering. Added to this were the anti-psychotic drugs that caused agitation, anxiety, insomnia, aggression, and irritation.

In a hospital there is always a rush at the end of each shift to get everything caught up. Dad became even more agitated and confused when he was rushed. He soon began striking out at staff and patients as he wandered in and out of rooms. Nurses would call the doctor for yet another injection of Haldol to calm him and control his activity and aggression because the previous injection hadn't worked. Added to the mix was the fact that a state hospital inspection was pending, which meant everyone was uptight and scurrying around trying to get everything prepared and perfect for the inspectors.

Dad became defensive. The more medication he had, the more difficult he was to handle. He peed on the floor by his bed and slipped and fell in it. The harder he was to control, the more tense and uptight the caregivers became. Dad picked up on their mood and became even more tense and uptight too. The situation became disastrous.

Valley View administration told us we would have to move him. They couldn't continue to deal with him in an acute care setting where other patients needed their attention, but they couldn't find a place to move him that would agree to accept him. The hospital patient coordinators were working with another hospital sixty-five miles away to see if he could be relocated to their long-term care facility. The answer was delayed while they had meetings to decide.

I left work the day I heard he was totally out of control and having a catastrophic reaction, which is what often happens when Alzheimer patients can't handle stressors and feel overloaded with too much activity. When I arrived at the hospital Dad was temporarily tied in a wheelchair. He had tried to escape. Like a speeding car chased by a highway patrolman, he had led a parade of people down the halls who were struggling to restrain him. He was given injections to sedate him, but nothing worked. As a result of all the commotion, his behavior became even more erratic and wild. Now they were dealing not only with his Alzheimer's, but also the drug interactions and side effects that caused the very thing they were trying to prevent. He was paranoid and aggressive and more confused than ever.

When I got there, I tried to calm him down. The staff was relieved to have a family member with him because they were at their wits' end. A nurse was attempting to orient him, "Ray, do you know where you are? Do you know what day it is?" I could see that her efforts were going nowhere because he was somewhere else. It reminded me of a similar situation when my son was three years old. A two-year-old hit him on the head with a hammer. The parents tried to reason with their toddler about why he shouldn't hit another child, instead of simply taking the hammer away. It is just as useless trying to reason with an Alzheimer's patient. Of course Dad couldn't tell the nurse where he was and what day it was.

As I led Dad down the hall toward a private waiting room to get him away from all the noise and confusion, he shouted at me, "If you interfere with the Forest Service when they are trying to fight a fire you could get court marshaled!" I followed him as he paced rapidly up and down the hall shouting, "Don't attract attention to us. I'd hate to be the guy that blocked the fire marshal!" He was drooling, a side effect of the drugs, and when I attempted to hand him a Kleenex he shouted at me, "What's wrong with you! Get that out of here! Don't you know that will kindle a fire?"

I could see that whatever Dad was imagining or reliving was very real to him. He was trembling, and his lip was quivering from fright. I led him into the unused private waiting room, and closed the door to shut out everything that was overloading his senses. I didn't try to constrain him. He was so upset, he talked nonstop for over an hour as I listened to him and responded calmly. Three hours later when I was sure he would fall asleep, I was able to open the door and lead him to his room and get him in bed.

I asked the nurse if she could give him his eight o'clock nightly meds a half hour early because I finally had him calmed down and almost asleep. She refused stating that hospital rules are not that flexible, and she couldn't do it. He fell into an exhausted sleep just as the nurse came in a half-hour later to wake him up for his eight o'clock meds. That only served to stir him up. Because hospitals are so regimented, he was awakened for meds and vitals according to their schedule rather than his need for sleep.

Later in the week, when I thought things were finally settled down, my mother called in tears, "He hasn't slept in two days and nights. He's uncontrollable, and no one can calm him." Things escalated to the point where he thought he was in a war zone, and he fought the staff. The more they tried to reason or restrain him, the more out of control he became. He slapped a nurse, punched two aides in the ribs, and clawed a ward clerk, yelling, "Someone is robbing me!" He refused any food or drink because " . . . it's been poisoned" and yelled that he would get a knife to slit their throats.

I wanted a way out of Dad's Alzheimer's, but there was no escaping. We were learning instead that God gives us a way though our problems. The same doctor who said he would make it work, threw up his hands in sheer frustration after one week and wrote in Dad's chart, "This patient is a danger to himself and others and needs to be physically and chemically restrained. Despite what state and federal regulations say, this patient requires sedation and restraints."

It was a week of constant ups and downs. The hospital called to say they had a place to transfer him and that we should come get him and move him to the new facility. As we were preparing to go they called back and said that the new facility had re-evaluated and refused to accept him. Then we received word that a second hospital would take him, but we would have to wait because there was no doctor who would accept him. They would know more by the following Monday.

Monday night I got a call from a nurse at Valley View who said it didn't seem right to send him away, they would move him to a quieter part of the facility. I went to bed praising God that it was settled, he would stay close to home. Then they called back on Tuesday and said we had to move him immediately, or they would send him to Redding by ambulance and charge us for the ride. The chief of staff had gotten involved and ordered him moved "before the state closes us down." They said Sun Valley Skilled Nursing Facility would take him. I knew Sun Valley had a reputation as a bottom-of-the-line facility, and I hated to think of Dad in that place, but it looked like we had no other choice.

Looking back at how he responded to different environments, I see that the setting was a key part of the problem. The techniques used at Valley View hospital were wrong. You can't expect an Alzheimer's patient to be calm in an environment that is anything but calm. Without stability chaos will prevail.

It's amazing how much an Alzheimer's patient can upset a facility. It's only natural for nurses and administration to want to do something that will calm and control the patient. But the first step ought to be to move the patient to a quieter room and decrease the amount of sensory stimulation. The pill or injection should be the last step, not the first. Side effects of medication can be like adding fuel to a fire when you're trying to get the fire to burn out.

Dad was in Valley View hospital for only a week, when much to the relief of the entire hospital staff, we picked him up for his move to back to Redding, seventy-five miles away. He was exhausted and agitated, but not out of control. Once he was in the car, he quieted down.

Sun Valley Skilled Nursing Facility was our last resort option, and we were looking for alternatives. When we got to Redding, we took him to see a psychiatrist. The psychiatrist said he was over medicated. After the examination, the doctor called a nurse who operated a placement service. He interviewed Dad and contacted area board-and-care homes that he felt would be most suitable. We hoped he was on the right track.

* * *

The nurse from the placement service interviewed Dad and suggested a private home, Village Home Care, thirty miles south of Redding. We stopped for dinner on the way and arrived in the evening. Shade trees lined the driveway, and the lawn was well kept. The atmosphere was friendly and homey and we were met and welcomed by the owner. We were pleased thinking Dad would do better out of the hectic city life in Redding.

As we entered the kitchen, four or five pleasant looking elderly ladies were sitting around the small oval kitchen table having tea. They seemed pleased to have a man joining them. The owner placed a chair for Dad at the table and handed him a cup of tea while we filled out the paperwork with her. Dad seemed to be enjoying the attention, but when it came time for us to go, the owner sensed our misgivings about leaving him in another strange place. To reassure us she said, "Don't you worry about a thing. He'll be just fine. I've had years of experience in this business. There's no Alzheimer patient I can't handle. In fact, I even wrote a manual on caregiving for them. Your dad is in good hands now." She proudly showed us her published care-giving guide full of answers for any situation. We said goodbye to Dad and he replied, "Thank you for coming."

When we got back in the car, we had to admit it was comforting knowing that at last we had found the right place for him, that he was in the hands of someone who was not only trained, but who specialized in caring for Alzheimer's patients. We were impressed that she had so much knowledge and experience. We stayed at my brother-in-law's overnight and slept peacefully knowing everything was under control, with a positive prospect for the future. Finally, a place for him. What a relief. We were especially grateful that he didn't have to go to Sun Valley, the end-of-the-line facility where hospitals sent patients who could not be accepted anywhere else.

The telephone woke us early the next morning. My brother-in-law leaned into our room and said, "The phone is for you, Edna. Sounds urgent."

I wondered who could be calling so early before we were out of bed. I barely had time to say hello when I was interrupted by the owner of Village Home Care: "You have to come get your dad right now. I will not put up with keeping him another minute. You won't believe the night I've had; it all started after you left. He threw a cup of tea and the teacup in a lady's face because she asked him not to take it away from the table. I want him out of here immediately." My dad was homeless again.

Even though it looked like things were going from bad to worse, how much worse could they get? If this was how 1998 was going to be, I wanted 1997 back. Yet, my theory has always been, just because God hasn't answered my prayer yet, doesn't mean he's not going to. I continued to believe that with God all things were possible.

I wanted to know what I could depend on when my world was falling apart. I watched others and saw the results of the advice they followed, good and bad. I watched to see if what they believed in worked. I didn't want it to be like the bald-headed drug rep who came into the medical center promoting a product for hair growth. Of course no one wanted to use his product. I didn't want to depend on something that didn't work. So many people sought advice from Ann Landers. People depended on her to tell them what to do, and they lived by her advice. I loved reading her column. She was solid and stood strong. Then I noticed her advice was changing. Previously she told her readers that marriage was forever, and couples should work out their problems. Then she started saying, "Throw the bum out." I lost faith in Ann Landers.

About that same time, I was given a handout in our emergency medical technician class. It was a protocol listing all the medications and interventions for cardiac arrhythmias. The instructor said, "This is your bible. Memorize it." The next day she said, "Oops, sorry, there was a misprint on a medication dose that could be fatal. Toss that." So much for our bible. In my nursing class, we were told that if we had any medical books over five-years-old to toss them out because they were no longer accurate. What we were taught as fact, five years later was now not only insignificant, but wrong. Each new study that came out in the news seemed to contradict another older one. I decided I wanted to search for truth that I could depend on because my brain was beginning to feel like a ping pong ball. One day the news would announce "Studies have proven . . . ," then in a few days that study would be refuted. I felt like a remote on a TV constantly being switched back and forth. For example, studies showed that caffeine is bad for you and detrimental to your health and could actually kill brain cells. Then a study came out saying that caffeine could actually increase memory. One study discounted the other. Another study showed that women need hormones after menopause. Later studies said hormones could increase chances of developing cancer. What was I supposed to believe?

I wanted advice that didn't change with each circumstance and generation. I finally discovered there was something in life I could depend on: the Bible. I found that when my whole world was changing, I could have faith in the one thing that doesn't. I learned that the only thing we can count on is God's word. We see results of it against overwhelming odds. I applied what I read in the Bible to life, just as I would try a new product to see if it worked. I started out by trusting the Bible for little things, just like my son-in-law Tony, who started climbing in a climbing gym instead of tackling Mount Everest.

Some people let past experiences of boredom keep them from reading the Bible. All of us have been in classes where the professor drones on and on, lecturing while people doodle on notepads and yawn to keep from falling asleep. It doesn't mean the topic is boring, it just means it has been presented that way. I read the Bible for myself and found what my neighbor told me to be true. She had been on a cruise and read *War and Peace*. After she finished it, she looked for something else to read and saw a Bible. She picked it up and read it from cover to cover. "I laughed. I cried," she said, "I realized there was not one part of life that it didn't touch. It was the most interesting book I had ever read."

So many times people in an overwhelming situation say, "All we can do is pray." I believe that prayer is not a last resort, with no results to hope for, but a first resort with answers. In my early twenties, I was with a friend at the house of an old lady who said she prayed for God to help her thread a needle whenever she sewed. We were shocked that anyone would pray for something so insignificant. We laughed to ourselves thinking, "Why would you bother God with something that small?" I recalled that incident when I was in my forties and had to get glasses and decided that wasn't such a dumb request after all.

I started praying for the small things as well as the big, and I discovered that prayer worked when I stopped complaining about the problems and instead focused on the promises I found in God's word. Now instead of a last resort, I turn to prayer first. In the same way that you come to trust a piece of equipment or a person's word. I learned what I could depend on and what I couldn't.

Once we bought a car that was loaded with options. The car had everything: leather interior, heated seats, dual control heater, the best stereo system, the OnStar program, and theft protection. The works. But we sold it because we couldn't depend on it to not die on us, especially when climbing difficult terrain when we needed it most. You can't trust a vehicle that fails you, even though it would start and run later. Supposedly it had a computer glitch. Through experience after experience I learned to put my faith in the one thing that doesn't change, doesn't fail, something I can always trust and depend on. I know God keeps his word.

After we were told Dad was no longer welcome at Village Home Care, I called my Aunt Lillian for comfort and support because I knew she was a woman of prayer. Three of my friends had lost their fathers in the last year, and Dad was still alive. But his life could barely be called living. I begged God to either calm him like he calmed the waves in the sea or take him.

I listened on the telephone while Aunt Lillian prayed, "Father God, you are the only source in the universe that hears and answers the heart cry of your people. You say in your word that you loose the prisoners. We pray that you will either deliver completely and free my brother Ray's mind from Alzheimer's or that you cut the silver cord of life and set his spirit free." I had never heard the term "the silver cord of life," but I found it in the Bible: "Remember your Creator now, before the silver cord of life is snapped apart . . . then shall the dust return to the earth as it was, and the Spirit shall return to God who gave it,"(Ecclesiastes 12: 6-7).

Before Alzheimer's, Dad would say, "Now if anything ever happens to me, I want you know I have a little savings in the bank in Redding." I answered, "I'm concerned about you, not just your money." He always responded, "Oh, don't worry about me, if there's a heaven, I'll get there somehow. I'm a good man, I've lived a good life, and I've never done anything wrong." Then he would always change the subject. "Enough of that. Now, let's go over to the Fireman's Carnival."

I knew Dad had made his peace with God after he became childlike. One day as he was sitting at my kitchen counter, I heard him pray, "I'm sorry Jesus." He finally came to the place where he admitted he might need Jesus to help him get to heaven. He had times of awareness when he knew his actions and attitudes were wrong. He knew he needed help and forgiveness. He was ready to admit he couldn't get to heaven just based on living right.

It had been a year since my first prayer that God would let me have Dad for one more year. I was now ready to let him go. I asked God now to set Dad free. I asked that if his time wasn't up yet that God take away the aggressiveness and combativeness. I prayed he would have peace of mind, and that we could find the right balance of medications, so that his behavior would be manageable. I believe that God is the one who determines how long a person lives. I felt better after praying and leaving it with God.

My husband said, "It's possible that Ray could live to be 104, like his mother, because he's still so strong physically." Lennie felt bad for my dad having to go through this torment when it was so contrary to his nature, and Lennie knew Dad never wanted to be a burden to anyone. He had heard Dad say so many times, "When it's my time, I want to go just like that," snapping his fingers for emphasis. We believed that God numbers our days and is the giver and taker of life. Because Dad was still alive, we believed there was a reason.

I wished that life was as simple as the Plumas Bank's slogan, "If you have a problem, we can help you." I often wondered how they would have handled it if I would have left Dad in their bank. No family member could help with Dad. And the doctor who said, "It'll work; we'll make it work," couldn't make it work. The psychiatrist/internist couldn't fix it. The placement nurse couldn't analyze it. And now the woman who had all the answers for Alzheimer's patients couldn't solve it.

*   *   *

We picked up Dad at from Village Home Care, and left the owner to write another chapter in her book on how to deal with Alzheimer's patients. Overnight she went from knowing all the answers, to being without an answer, adding to the trail of facilities and caregivers who were relieved to see us drive away with Dad and his belongings.

We took Dad to Sun Valley, the only place that would accept him due to the statement by our local doctor on Dad's discharge summary: "This man is a danger to himself and others and needs to be physically and chemically restrained involuntarily in a locked facility."

We parked near the sign that read Sun Valley Skilled Nursing Facility. Dad walked without assistance and willingly followed us up the long flight of stairs to his new home. The entrance was ordinary and rather benign. This facility was older than the others, well worn, with faded, out-dated furniture in the reception area. A yellow cat was perched on a large fish tank with one paw dangling down into the murky green algae, hoping to catch an unsuspecting fish.

The busy receptionist put the phone on hold and greeted us from behind her cluttered metal desk. Mother handed her Dad's insurance cards and completed the clipboard of necessary paperwork. An aide came to show Dad to his room.

What a shock as we turned the corner. It was as if we had just entered the on-ramp to a freeway. There was an onslaught of sights and sounds: a mad rush of food carts, laundry carts, delivery people, and visitors dodging the residents as they wandered in all directions. Overhead announcements filled the air, "Good morning. Today is Wednesday, January 7, 1998. We will have bingo at 3:30 in the activities room." The constant ringing of phones at the nurse's station added to the commotion. The smell of stale urine permeated the air as we walked down the hall, and the odor of feces emanated from the overfilled wet, dirty laundry bags hanging out of the baskets that lined the hallway. In the hallway, residents were cussing, crying, and yelling things like "Help me! Somebody help me." They reached out to us or tried to grab us as we passed. Some were staring straight ahead with vacant, detached looks on their faces. Others peered curiously at us. Some residents made eye contact and appeared alert. Others sat motionless and unaware of our presence. Elderly people pushed by in walkers or shuffled by with canes. Aides were scurrying from room to room as call bells buzzed nearly constantly.

We passed one eccentric-looking lady with rumpled, unkempt hair wearing mismatched clothes and sitting in a wheelchair. My mother, in an attempt to be friendly, smiled at the woman. In response, the woman let out a string of profanity ending with, " . . . and you can stuff it up your ass." Mother recoiled in shock. The beauty operator leaned out of the door of her shop and warned, "Watch out; she bites too!"

As we continued down the hall and turned left into the room that Dad had been assigned, we passed by Norton, his former roommate at our local hospital, who was still in constant motion. Norton had beaten us to Sun Valley because he had been transported from Valley View by ambulance the day before.

Dad's room looked like an old version of a college dormitory with three beds to a room. The man in the bed next to the door, though he was unable to speak and was paralyzed, was able to nod "yes" or "no" to our questions. The man in the middle bed was curled up in a fetal position. There was a small pool of fresh blood in the center of his bed. Dad was assigned to the bed near the window that looked out onto the brick wall of the next building.

The aide showed Mother where to put Dad's belongings. Mother put his clothes in his closet while the aide filled out the admission forms. After the aide finished weighing Dad and taking his vitals, it was time to eat. We went together to the dining room. We left him there and went to meet with the interdisciplinary team. My mother was glad his care would be supervised by this team from every department. She requested that Dad have physical therapy to strengthen his muscles. She was concerned that he was losing muscle tone. Because he was a tall man, Mother felt he needed more calories than the frail, elderly ladies. The nutritionist promised her that he would be given larger portions.

Dad seemed to be adapting all right so we left for the two-hour drive home. My mother was elated that he was in a skilled nursing facility because the care would be carefully monitored. It also meant that she and Dad would finally qualify for reimbursement from Dad's long-term care insurance and would no longer have to pay all his expenses out of their own pockets. We were also grateful that a physician had agreed to accept Dad there. I was slightly apprehensive about the whole environment but didn't want to dampen my mother's enthusiasm. I wondered about the awareness level of the aide who was caring for Dad. She asked me if I was his wife. I kept my misgivings about Sun Valley to myself.

In the days and nights that followed, Dad was understandably confused and disoriented. He was in another facility with strangers and nothing was familiar. He wandered in and out of resident's rooms, which resulted in numerous complaints especially if he crawled into a bed to take a nap without noticing it was already occupied.

Almost immediately, my mother started receiving calls that Dad had fallen. The facility was required to notify families of any fall. The calls increased to daily reports that he had fallen. This seemed unusual because he was physically healthy and normally steady on his feet. My mother would no sooner hang up the phone from calling me to tell me he had fallen, when her phone would ring again reporting yet another fall. I was suspicious. I knew that patients fall not just because they are elderly and feeble but because they are over medicated.

We took Dad for his regularly scheduled appointment with Dr. Donner, the internist/psychiatrist. Dad was wobbly and unsteady on his feet. Drool flowed from his mouth, down his chin, and onto his shirt. Dr. Donner examined him and said Dad was dehydrated and over-medicated. He sent an order to Sun Valley to decrease the dosage of his psychotropic medications.

A week later, we received a call from the nurse at Dr. Donner's office. The doctor wondered why they had received a request from the pharmacy for Dad's Zyprexia refill when the he himself had ordered it discontinued. He said he would contact Dad's newly assigned physician. The mistake was caught by Dr. Donner's nurse because their office had been seeing Dad on a consistent basis throughout the time he was in and out of numerous facilities. Since Dad had been moved frequently and had to use different pharmacies, the mistake went unnoticed by the pharmacy requesting the refill. It was no wonder that Dad had been falling.

The medication had been building up in his system. Instead of being given a reduced dosage, he was given more medication on top of what was already in his system. Because of my mother's careful documentation, we once again could see the patterns of the medication buildup. Once the medication was discontinued, he was walking without assistance again. His confusion decreased, and his behavior gradually improved. I agree with Dr. Robbins, Director of the Colorado Geriatric Education Center: "Topping the differential diagnosis for confusion are medications, medications, medications."

Physical therapy for muscle strengthening had been ordered, but instead of being followed through on, it backfired. When I asked why Dad was no longer walking, the aides told us they were not allowed to walk him. "Once physical therapy is ordered, he can only be walked by the physical therapy department and they're not available." So his muscles became weaker as he lay in bed. It seemed so many of the promises at Sun Valley got lost in the process, as paperwork became the priority instead of the patient's well being.

Another problem for the caregivers was Dad's "politeness." He liked to help little old ladies up out of their wheelchairs. The problem was two-fold. Some of the wheelchair occupants could not get up, and others did not want to get up. If Dad was unsuccessful at helping the woman out of her wheelchair, he would shake the wheelchair until it rattled trying to jar it, loose. This alarmed the elderly ladies to the point of being seriously frightened and calling for help. Attempting to reason with Dad was a waste of time.

The nursing staff tried to keep him out of residents' rooms by putting him in a closed chair made of white PVC pipes. It was more like a tall cage than a chair. It was designed to be awkward enough to block the doorways and keep him from going through. We were notified that if this did not work, we would have to move him because other residents continued to complain about Dad's behavior.

We were told at the next committee meeting that the PVC chair had failed. Dad somehow had managed to maneuver it through the doorways into the rooms and was still agile enough to climb out of it. One time I stopped him and made him back up out of a room into the hallway. I was trying to avoid a confrontation between him and another resident. I said, "You can't stay in here."

He replied, "Then where can I play?"

Once again, the staff resorted to chemical restraints, a temporary fix causing long-term problems. The medication had a positive effect at first and then compounded the negative behavior. Some of the side effects were the very symptoms the drugs were meant to prevent. His confusion and agitation increased, and he became even more difficult to manage. His increased weakness was directly proportional to his increased medication.

The next time I went to visit Dad he looked like he had aged ten years. He was unsteady on his feet and almost tripped himself when he walked. Soon he was unable to walk without assistance. Once again, when we inquired, we discovered his medication level had been increased, and we saw the familiar pattern all over again. He became a fall risk. Soon he was in a wheelchair again, even though two weeks earlier he had walked unaided down the hall. He pushed himself along with his feet and responded weakly to us saying, "I'm tired. I want to go home."

Mother received a call that Dad had attempted to stand up and had fallen out of his wheelchair. The nurse said that he was falling because he forgets to lock the wheelchair. He didn't fall because he forgot to lock the wheelchair; he was incapable of knowing or remembering that he needed to lock the wheelchair. One time I found him in a wheelchair pulling himself slowly down the hall by grasping the hand railing. All he could say was "Don't feed it. Leave it all in space."

Dad had not known me for months. My prayer was that he would know me once again. I prayed he would call me Edna May. I had to admit, I was a little jealous that he always recognized Lennie, but it was hard to know whether it was Lennie or the baseball cap he wore that got Dad's attention. I prayed that that he would again have that spark of recognition in his eyes. Four months later, on April 26, 1998, when I walked in the door at Sun Valley my dad was in the hallway. He turned to the lady next to him and said, "There's my daughter!"

I asked him, "Do you know my name?"

He answered, "Edna May. Funny we should meet in a place like this."

The ups and downs were difficult. I think the hardest part for us was thinking that Dad had adjusted and was doing well at each facility and then the huge let down when it all fell apart. As I write this, I relive the disappointment, and I wonder why we didn't intervene more. Each time we felt we had found the answer. Each time something gave us hope that this would be the place, this would be the solution. For example at Sun Valley we thought, finally, we have found a place where they can manage him. If an inter-disciplinary team is handling it, we have the combined wisdom of every department focusing on his care. Previously it was the physician telling us he thought he had found the right balance of his medications. Or the lady who wrote the book on Alzheimer's telling us she knew exactly how to handle him. The string of events had us feeling like we were on an airport conveyor belt moving us forward, and we couldn't jump off.

When I wanted to call it quits and bring Dad home, something would happen to show us it would not work. One night I went to bed at seven-thirty because I was so physically and emotionally exhausted and slept until seven in the morning. Lennie said that proved that I couldn't have cared for Dad at home.

We had to accept that we had no choice. Nothing we had done and nothing anyone else had done had worked. We had no alternatives to Sun Valley. We couldn't care for him. No one else could really care for him properly either. And absolutely no one would take him back. It was the mid-1990s, and there were no other options available then. Now Alzheimer's facilities allow residents to wander in a safe, controlled environment with combinations on the doors that are too complicated for them to open. Now people have more understanding of patients with Alzheimer's disease. Then, care and treatment was in the more experimental stages.

Our visits to Dad were always the same routine. First we'd find him and see how he was doing. Many days it wasn't very good. How could a man be capable of driving all over Europe in World War II now have no idea how to put one foot in front of the other without being told? I'd usually have to go into his room to find his hearing aids because they were never in his ears. His glasses were usually missing too. Each time we came we had to sort through a box of tangled glasses in the lost and found. To deal with that, we ordered Dad some new, easily identifiable bright red glasses and put his name on them. After we'd get him situated with his hearing aids and glasses, then we'd try to locate his missing slippers and clothes.

I hated this facility and its malfunctioning interdisciplinary teams. They made all kinds of promises to my mother about Dad's care, promises that sounded good on paper, but were never followed through. I always found out more from Dad's roommate, who could speak only through gestures, than I did from the nurses. Each time I went to see Dad in January that year, I was frustrated. There were no regular nurses or aides. Any time I would inquire about him, the person I asked would say, "I don't know, I'm only weekend help" or "Ask someone else," or "I don't know, I'm only part time." One time an aide taking his vitals told me his pulse rate had been running "eighteen to twenty." Even Lennie knew that had to be his respirations not his pulse. It didn't even register with her when she said it.

The next time I visited, Dad had bruises and scratch marks on his inner, upper arms in the shape of fingernails dug into his skin. When I asked the aide about the marks, he said he had to hold Dad back from getting in a fight with another resident. Not an acceptable explanation. On a visit shortly after that, we were told by the aides that his red glasses and one of his hearing aids were missing. We were never able to find them.

It was so hard to see Dad in such terrible condition in a place where all the committee's promises of extra nutrition, physical therapy, and specialized care were not carried out. When we scheduled an appointment at the hearing aid center, we had to cancel it because his ears were full of wax and hair. Each time we were told that Sun Valley needed a doctor's order before they could clean his ears and each time the order was never obtained or followed up on so we had to postpone yet another appointment.

Once I called and said, "This is Ray Methvin's daughter and I would like to know how my dad is doing." The nurse replied, "Oh she's doing fine." Another time we found Dad in the dining room at meal time. He was doing his usual routine of attempting to pull himself up by hanging onto the table and then plopping back down in his chair multiple times. His food was untouched. A fellow resident hollered from across the dining hall, "Don't let him leave the table because he won't get any more food until tomorrow."

Finally we figured out some of the mealtime problems. Residents were given a choice, to eat in their room or the dining room. Dad was incapable of choosing, so he missed a lot of meals when the aides thought he was in the other room. He had reached the point where he was unable to eat without assistance. Because there were 300 residents and not enough aides, his tray was consistently taken away with most of the food untouched after overworked aides offered him a couple of bites and gave up. Without help and encouragement, he barely ate at all. At my mother's request, the dietitian reviewed the food consumption records, which were not always accurate. For instance, an aide I knew told me she was fired for eating food off of a resident's tray. Dad was given a snack of ice cream, but because he couldn't eat it without assistance, it was left melting on his tray until it was taken away and documented "refused." His weight continued to decline.

One time when I went to see Dad, I sat in the dining room with him before mealtime, and I witnessed a scene that will always remain in my mind. After a half hour wait, the residents who were coherent and capable picked up their spoons and started banging them on the table chanting louder and louder, "We want food! We want food!" The food that came was white bread covered with white gravy that had tiny specks of meat in it, if you looked closely. The dessert was chocolate pudding. Dad started spreading chocolate pudding all over his bread as if it were jelly, and then ate it with his fingers. I smiled because my mother had always been so formal at dinner, practicing the etiquette she had learned as a home economics major. If Dad spilled anything on his shirt or missed a spot on his face, she always corrected him. Now Alzheimer's let him enjoy dessert first, and if he ate chocolate pudding on top of gravy on bread who cared?

Once my mother received a call that Dad had slipped and fallen out of his wheel chair and that the maintenance man was passing by and found him. Lennie wondered out loud what kind of care he was receiving if it was the maintenance man who found him. There was a high turnover of staff at Sun Valley. Because the pay at this facility was so low, qualified caregivers moved on to better paying jobs. It takes a special person to be an aide, willing to wipe butts, clean up vomit, give bed baths, do heavy lifting, and change wet and poopy clothes.

Dad had always referred to water as "God's brew," yet on each shift his bedside water pitcher was emptied and refilled, and he was not offered a drink. In his mental condition, he was unable to seek it out for himself. One aide told me that she quit another facility because they were trying to reduce overhead by cutting back on food. Residents who had to be fed pureed food were only getting pureed white bread and water. By the end of January, after being at Sun Valley a little over one month he had lost sixteen pounds. We wished we lived close enough to go in and help at mealtimes, but we lived two hours away. By Valentines Day, Dad's weight was down to 135 pounds.

He could no longer eat without assistance and encouragement, and as a result, he missed many meals. He had lost thirty pounds in two months at Sun Valley. Dad was six-foot-two and now weighed the same as I did. It made no sense, and there was no excuse for it. We were attending meetings about his nutritional status, and the staff said they were making good progress. He had a supply of bananas—his favorite food—that my mother left for him at his bedside, but they were untouched and black because they were not offered to him. The home-baked cookies weren't eaten because he had lost the basic instinct to seek out food when he was hungry. He had changed from being tempted by food and naturally hungry to having it in front of him and not reaching for it unless it was handed to him. Lack of proper nutrition affected him not only physically but mentally.

This situation reminded me of my mother's best friend who had been diagnosed with Alzheimer's. My mother called her at home and asked if she had eaten, and Ouida went to the refrigerator to see if the food was still there. When she was in the hospital for a just week getting the proper nutrition, her mental function significantly improved. Many of the prescriptions Dad was taking lowered his appetite, inhibited his ability to taste, and increased his confusion, with the combined result of decreased overall nutrition and weight loss.

During this period, the staff at Sun Valley kept requesting increases in Dad's medications because of behavior problems, until one day I found him looking down at the wheelchair he was sitting in repeating over and over again, "I wouldn't buy this chair if I was you. This chair isn't comfortable." I knew this was Dad's way of complaining of pain because he repeated it and could not be distracted. I knew there was something wrong because he never complained of pain. He had always had his teeth filled without Novocain. I asked the speechless man in the bed by the door to nod as I held up fingers so I would know how many days my dad had been like this. One.

My mother had received a call that he had slipped and fallen from his wheelchair. The nurses told me he was found on the floor after he climbed over the bedrail. I asked if an X-ray had been done. They said the on-call doctor had ordered one and it was negative. I requested another one because Dad was in pain and couldn't stand. They reluctantly contacted his regular doctor for an order. They did a second X-ray, and it showed he had a displaced fracture of the right pelvis. They wanted me to sign papers giving my permission for a lap buddy or lap table to attempt to keep him in the wheelchair as treatment for the fracture.

As I was signing the consent papers for the lap buddy, the med nurse was approaching the door of his room with her medication cart. I asked her to withhold the doses of Respirital, Ativan, and Buspar, saying, "He has fallen twice because he was overmedicated, and you're giving him more?" I wanted to talk to the doctor on call, and the med nurse said it would do no good because he was not familiar with Dad's case. I said to her, "If I have to give my permission for you to start him on these meds in order to sedate him enough to keep him out of other patient's rooms then, I can withdraw my permission when he is so obviously overmedicated and is only a danger to himself."

I had no idea what a stir I created until the next day at work when I received a call from the charge nurse, the administrator, and the social services director all telling me that I could not do what I had done. Dad's doctor called me and admitted Dad was overmedicated and apologized. He also warned me that this facility had a reputation for releasing patients without warning and to be prepared because they were contacting other facilities.

Dad's doctor said there are behavior cycles with Alzheimer's patients and that their behavior changes depending on whether they perceive their environment as frightening or friendly. Alzheimer's patients often don't correctly perceive or interpret stimuli coming at them, and they become defensive and react accordingly. It isn't predictable when their behavior changes will occur because the cycling is due to both internal functions and their environment.

When I called the next day to see how Dad was, the nurse said "no change." I wondered if that was good or bad. The medication change didn't work; the lap chair didn't work; they wanted him out of there; and no one would accept him. We had come up with no solutions on our own, so I left it up to God because he fights our battles for us. Finally I accepted this as a "Red Sea situation." There would be no answer unless God parted the sea or moved mountains.

At least the uncertainty about Dad staying at Sun Valley was gone. The administrator made it clear: he wanted Dad out of there. The only question was, where would he go? My husband still felt it would not work to put a mobile home on our property and hire caregivers. A new facility was opening in Williams between Redding and Sacramento. We called and they said they would accept him, but they wouldn't open for several months.

Dad 's future remained uncertain. We thought of the verse that says, "Take no thought about tomorrow," (Matthew 6:34). I gave Dad's tomorrows to God and asked that he cause the people in charge of choosing or rejecting residents to do so as evidence that Dad would be in the best possible place.

It was frustrating to us that instead of trying to eliminate or investigate the causes of Dad's acting out, the staff at Sun Valley just added another prescription in an attempt to chemically restrain him, when the cause for his behavior may have been as simple as a bladder infection. A nurse I worked with had an infant son who was screaming uncontrollably in the middle of the night and could not be consoled. She thought maybe he had been bitten by a spider or yellow jacket but could find no sign of a bite. She went to the medical center to borrow an otoscope to look in his ears to try to determine what was wrong. When she returned home, the baby was cooing and smiling in her husband's arms. She looked puzzled at the change in him. Her husband said, "Oh, he farted and now he's fine." The baby couldn't communicate what was wrong. Some Alzheimer's patients have no better means of communicating than this baby did, but they receive a long-term solution—another regimen of pills—to solve a temporary problem.

In EMT (emergency medical technician) training, we learned to look for the simplest cause first. In emergencies medical personnel are taught BLS before ALS: basic life support before advanced life support. We all have basic needs for oxygen, water, food, elimination, security, and love. An Alzheimer's patient may be thirsty, hungry, bored, or simply need redirection. Often in Dad's case, he was dehydrated because he was not offered water, and he was unable to seek it out on his own. Dehydration triggers a cascade of physical and mental symptoms. I am sure his nursing care documentation included "thought process altered, memory deficit," "self care deficit," "nutrition altered, less than body requirements," "high risk for fluid volume deficit." It looked good on paper. But all he needed was for someone to hand him a glass of water or see that he ate what was in front of him. A prescription for agitation does not solve the problem when the real solution is taking the time to find the cause of the disruptive behavior in the first place. It is vitally important to find and address the cause or change the environment that triggered the disruptive behavior.

Once his medication was reduced and his fractured pelvis mended, my dad was walking without assistance. He smiled and kissed mother and called her by name. And when it was raining when we got out of the car for his next psychiatric appointment, he held the umbrella for her.

* * *

At the end of April, Dad's doctor at Sun Valley warned me again that the facility had a reputation for releasing patients without warning. Expecting

142 Edna Eades, RN

the worst, we continued to look for an alternative. In May, the social services director confided to me that my dad's behavior had improved, and that they had quit actively looking for another place for him.

But at the end of May, my mother received a call from a director at Sun Valley saying that the placement service had been there, and they had found Dad a new facility. Mother told her that we wanted to look at it before he was moved. It turned out that two facilities in Redding were recommended.

My mother and I looked at both of them. One was a maze of hallways and doors, several long buildings that had been converted into one facility. This may have worked for us earlier, but Dad's Alzheimer's was too far advanced. If he couldn't find the bathroom or dining room in his own home, how could he find his way around in such a huge facility? The second place would have been perfect, but it was near a freeway and the door to outside was propped open with a rock. There was no fence, and because Dad wandered, he could have easily walked into the middle of four lanes of traffic.

Mother and I had driven down to Redding after I got off work, and it was late by the time we got back to Burney. We hadn't thought about restaurants being closed and were relieved to find that the pizza parlor had an "open" sign in the window. It was almost ten o'clock, and we were hungry and tired. As we got out of the car, we saw a hand reach out and turn the sign to "closed." We drove on to Fall River. When Mother said, "Where will we eat?" I said, "Simple. At whatever place is open." She talked about my dad's situation and how his future seemed so uncertain. "Where can he stay if they make him leave Sun Valley?" I told her he was in the same situation as we were at the moment, that he'll stay "at whatever place is open to him." We were getting used to facilities being "open" and then after they learned about Dad's history, having the "closed" sign go up instead.

But we continued to search, remembering that Dad had been willing to search the bottom of the deep and treacherous Pit One Canyon when my brother was missing. While my mother contacted more facilities by phone, Lennie and I drove to Roseburg, Oregon, to check out yet another.

As we headed north, my thoughts wandered to when I was in college. Two instructors stood out in my mind. Both of them had pat answers for everything. One always said, "Now that would be a good thing for you to look up." The other's pat answer to any concern was, "Not my problem." Although I was not impressed with their teaching techniques, their phrases stuck with me. I decided that God had to be more compassionate than either instructor and came to the conclusion that if he had not provided us with an answer or a way out of our dilemma, then he must be providing a way through. I again remembered the verse, "Take no thought for tomorrow," (Matthew 6:34).

I have seen lots of babies delivered and probably not one delivery where the mother didn't want to call it quits and go home, but in the end of course, the mothers were thankful that they saw it through. I knew we had to see this process through, too.

The Roseburg facility was new and looked like it would be ideal. They were willing to accept Dad but had no openings and a lengthy waiting list. We added his name to the list. On the way home we stopped at a veteran's geriatric-psychiatric ward. They refused him. "He doesn't qualify. We are very selective of our patients." I thought if he doesn't qualify for an elderly psychiatric veteran's facility, what does he qualify for?

I continued to pray that the right facility would be open to Dad, and that we would know it was the right one, because all the others would be closed. The lyrics, "God will make a way when there seems to be no way," kept going through my mind. I was saddened to think that all my dad ever wanted was a home and now there was not one place open to him. I read this verse, "The Lord will show us the way that we may walk and the thing that we may do," (Jeremiah 42:3).

When we got home we got a call from the Roseville facility saying they would accept him but that they were not opening until July. It was only May, and we didn't think that the people at Sun Valley would be willing to wait that long. We called for placement in Nevada, Oregon, and Central California. The most common response was "No one is available to take your call. Please leave a message." The second most common message was "The number you have dialed is disconnected and no longer in service." If I got a real person they said, "We have no openings. We are not able to help you." When I dialed one number I heard "J.C. Auto Parts. Can I help you?" I thought even though it was an obvious wrong number, at least they were willing to help and could probably take care of him as well as anyone else at this point.

My mother liked a facility in Klamath Falls. We applied. They required a hospital discharge report from Dad's most recent hospitalization. When they saw "This man is a danger to himself and others." they called my mother. "Under no circumstances and in no uncertain terms will we even consider taking him here."

The dreaded news from Sun Valley came at the beginning of June. "You have to move your dad. This time he threatened a female patient. He was in his wheelchair and moved toward her with a clenched fist. She fell back into a corner and screamed for help. We will call the cops if you don't come get him today. We found a facility for him, and it's not our fault if you don't like it." Sun Valley gave us twenty-four hours or less to move him. They claimed they had previously given us notice. We had nothing in writing and were under the impression they were still continuing to try to make it work. We were at the end of the road. Dad was at the end-of-the-line facility. Yet even they refused to keep him, and no other facility would accept him because they all required a hospital discharge summary. Because the doctor had written that Dad was a danger to himself and others, no one would accept him. Mother couldn't care for him at home any longer. My husband and I were both working and couldn't take him. We were at rock bottom with nowhere to turn. I had no brothers or sisters to call and say, "Your turn."

I called my mother and she cried. "What are we going to do now?" Here we were again, like the game boards that say "Go back two spaces. Do not pass go." We were back to square one. The local radio station I was listening to when I got home from work was playing a new song. I caught only one phrase, "When you have done all that you can do, stand." I had no plan so, as I have done before, I sought God through prayer and reading his word until something stood out to me. As I read Matthew 3:9, my eyes fell on "God is able." I wondered exactly what "able" involved so I looked it up in the Greek. It was "dunamis," meaning power, ability, strength. Those words shifted my focus off our problems and onto God's ability.

I realized that while we were powerless and had no strength to care for Dad or find a place for him, what was impossible with us was possible with God. Instead of giving up, we continued to comb California and the adjoining states looking for a facility, just as I knew my dad would have done for me if the roles were reversed.

When I didn't see the answer, I realized it was all about timing. I believed that just because he hadn't answered, it didn't mean God wasn't answering; it wasn't the right time yet. One day when I was working in the garden, I accidentally dug up a pea plant. It was spring and nothing had popped though the surface of the ground yet, but underneath there were roots being established. The seedlings just hadn't appeared. Similarly, in my dad's situation, something was in the process and would come to pass; we just couldn't see the results yet. Prayer is like that. We think nothing is happening because we can't see it, and all the while behind the scenes and under the surface, unseen progress is being made. I believed that God was directing our steps. "I will instruct you and teach you in the way that you should go," (Psalms 32:8).

*   *   *

After we got the ultimatum notice from Sun Valley, I tried the Alzheimer's Association in Lodi. I was in tears, and after that I couldn't bring myself to call any more facilities because I was crying so much. My husband contacted a facility in Medford, Oregon, that we had visited on our previous trip to Roseberg. We had not considered this facility after our previous trip because Mother wanted to wait to hear from the facility in Klamath Falls because she liked it and wanted him closer to home. Lennie explained everything to the administrator of the Medford facility. He told her that the people in charge at Sun Valley said they would call the cops if we didn't move him that day. She said, "That is the most ridiculous thing I have ever heard." She requested the phone number for Sun Valley. Then she called Lennie back and repeated what Sun Valley had told her: "We've never had a problem with him; he's just not suited for this facility." Then she said, "Bring him to Medford. We'll accept him."

Back to square one. When we picked Dad up he was in a wheel chair again and chemically restrained. We gathered what was left of his things that were not misplaced or lost, and the Sun Valley staff was quite willing to help us out the door. During the five-hour drive to Medford, we stopped at a rest area. My mother went into the women's bathroom, and I had to take my dad in his wheelchair to the men's and change him while Lennie stood outside the door. I worked as a nurse's aide for ten years and cleaned up a lot of patients, but it was way different having to take care of my own father. When you have no choice, you do what you think you can't.

We arrived at Mountain Manor Assisted Living in Medford without any disruptive incidents. Mountain Manor was a beautiful facility with walkways and well kept lawns adjoining the buildings. It was made up of several small, identical buildings and looked like a beautiful retirement home. There were only twelve patients assigned to a building. The use of smaller buildings eliminated noise and confusion and created a quiet, peaceful setting. There were combinations on entry doors to prevent residents from leaving on their own, but no maze of halls and doorways. My dad responded positively to the staff and appeared to like it there, but again, he wouldn't stay until they had invited him.

Mountain Manor was different, and Dad's behavior changed immediately. He wasn't lost in the shuffle of the typical hospital floor plan. Gone were the constant overhead announcements or the freeway of staff and residents, like wild brushes in a car wash coming at him simultaneously from all directions.

There was a program and a schedule. Activities were organized and supervised to keep the residents occupied. Residents were encouraged to participate. The only program the activities director was unsuccessful at getting Dad involved in was Bingo. He adamantly stated, "I don't smoke and I don't drink and I don't gamble!" Just like when he was in the military.

Wandering was encouraged instead of restricted. There was a circle to wander inside each building and another circular walk outside. The outside circle was in a walled yard with grass and flowers and in plain view of the caregivers. The walkway led in and out of the dining room, so residents couldn't get lost. They had a safe place to wander and nowhere else to go but back inside. Residents were able to find their rooms by pictures hanging at their doorways of themselves at a younger age. As the medication was reduced Dad was again steady on his feet and could wander as much as he wanted without getting lost or being restricted or restrained.

The staff was paid higher wages. There was little or no turnover. The aides knew each resident by name. Dad had consistent care by people who knew his habits and needs, likes and dislikes. The physician who accepted him was excellent and agreed that he needed to be tapered off his medications. For the first time, staff would be able to deal with the Alzheimer's instead of Alzheimer's plus the side effects and interactions of the drugs. When Dad was first admitted, I worried they wouldn't keep him because he was peeing in the corners of the rooms. When I mentioned my concern to my mother's neighbor she said, "That's okay, I understand. I'm having the same trouble with my new puppy." The staff was understanding, too. As his medication was reduced and a bathroom routine established, his incontinence stopped, and he was able to quit wearing Depends. That was a definite improvement.

Dad was served well-balanced meals with plenty of healthy food. Meals were consistent and supervised. His plate was not snatched away before he was finished, and there were not a lot of distractions to keep him from eating. He was given direction, and he was not expected to eat on his own. These improvements in his condition happened at a time when he was considered to be in the later stages of Alzheimer's. He should have been declining, but instead he began to improve. And he gained back the thirty pounds he had lost at Sun Valley.

Mountain Manor was three hours away from home, which meant we could only visit once a week. The first time I called to ask about him, I was told, "Oh, he's doing great. He is a delight to have. He meets another man in the hall and they shake hands and walk together."

I said, "Maybe you didn't hear the name correctly. This is Ray Methvin I'm calling about."

The person on the other end replied, "Yes, I know."

Could this be the same man who was declared a danger to himself and others and removed from the last three facilities?

Another time I was told he was "doing wonderfully and a pleasure to have around." One day when I visited, a staff member told me, "He has the kindest eyes of anyone I have ever known." Slowly we began to believe the reports that he was getting along well with others and not causing any problems for the staff. Since his environment was no longer threatening, he settled in, and his behavior changed.

Without the psychotropic drugs he was much more alert. My mother noted, "They care about Ray, not just his past behavior." When Mother and I visited in July, about a month after Dad's admission, he said, "That's Edna May with you isn't it?" He knew me for the first time in months. We all agreed we could not have found a better place for him.

In this facility, I could wash the wax out of his ears without a doctor's order. As I washed and cleaned his ears with a bulb syringe, warm water, and hydrogen peroxide, he said, "It feels like someone shitting in my ear." He was certainly there, "in the moment." He could hear better without all the hair and wax. His glasses were cleaned and placed on him daily, so his vision was better too. From the design of the facility, to the orderly routines, to the quiet atmosphere, to the professional and caring personnel, the focus and objectives were the same: the care, mental and physical well-being, and comfort of the residents.

But by August, a couple months after his admission, I sensed a withdrawing. As fall approached, his eyes seemed more distant. His color wasn't as good as it had been. My mother still felt he would outlive her by many years, but I wondered. I tried to explain my feelings to her, but I was unable to put what I was sensing into words. Then she described it perfectly: "fading."

I was grateful for his time at Mountain Manor, because I had my dad again, and not the out of control, unmanageable person he had been in the last three facilities. His previous caregivers expected him to change when all that was needed was a change in his environment and reduction in medication.

When I arrived in mid-September, he was sitting at a table in a wheelchair; previously he had been up walking without assistance. I asked why and the caregivers said that another man had hit him with his fist, and Dad was found on the floor. When the staff went running in, my dad just looked at them and asked, "Well, aren't you going to help me up?" One of the male aides who had been taking care of him liked to spar around with the older men, prancing around like a boxer and saying, "Put up your dukes." Maybe that's what started it, but since it wasn't witnessed, no one will ever know. All we could do was deal with the result.

I was relieved to know that my dad had not instigated the incident. I asked the staff if the laws were different in Oregon regarding notification of family because previously we were contacted every time he fell. I asked the director in charge of his unit why we weren't called and he replied, "We should have contacted you, but most families dissociate themselves when they place their family members in a rest home, and feel that it is not their father or mother anymore."

He had been taken to the emergency department four days before because he had complained of increasing pain and made fewer attempts to walk. The X-rays revealed a compression fracture of his back, but they diagnosed it incorrectly as an old injury.

I asked Dad to point to where it hurt and he pointed to his right abdominal quadrant in front and I thought he was just confused.

Neither I or the staff realized he had an undiagnosed gall bladder problem. At that time, we thought he had a back injury and expected him to point to his back. As it finally turned out, he was not confused at all. I asked him to stand, and when he attempted to walk, he collapsed immediately into his wheelchair. When I returned two days later, he was worse. My mother had been visiting her sister in Sacramento, and we made arrangements for her to come directly to Medford.

I took Dad to Provision Hospital by ambulance because he could not walk, and he cried out in pain with any movement. I knew something was terribly wrong because he had a strong pain threshold. The X-rays of his hip and pelvis were negative, so the radiologist suggested he be seen in again in the emergency room.

The doctors could find no cause that would explain why he was going downhill so fast. Because the exam and X-rays revealed nothing but the compression fracture of his back, they realized it had been wrongly diagnosed as an old injury. He was returned to Mountain Manor for six weeks of bed rest. We determined that Dad would be better off in the familiar surroundings of Mountain Manor because hospitalization would have a negative effect on him mentally. I thought it was so unfair that he should have a fractured back just four months after suffering the fractured pelvis at Sun Valley.

After a few days back at Mountain Manor, he was less responsive and had a temperature. I prayed, "Lord, I commit him to you. If you are ready to take him home, I'm ready to let him go." Once again, I found myself bargaining with God, asking that my dad be restored mentally and physically better than before, or that God would let him leave this world. It was an all or nothing prayer, either for God to improve him or set his spirit free and not to prolong his life the way it had been the last few years.

Dad was starting to get some skin breakdown on his heel, and I prayed that there would be no bedsores. His heel improved but the situation worsened. He fought the caregivers who were trying to keep him on bed rest. His temperature continued to climb. The doctor ordered antibiotics and IV's and home health. His level of response decreased.

By about a week after his return to Mountain Manor from the emergency room, he responded only enough to say, "I'm in a hell-of-a-fix, and I don't know what to do about it. I want to go home. Do I have to stay here?" He stopped swallowing and was dehydrating. The doctor wanted to know his code status, and we told him Dad had a standard "Directive to Physicians" that said that if at any time he had an incurable disease or illness that he wanted nothing done to prolong his life.

My mother leaned over his bed to tell him goodbye. Suddenly she raised up and said, "Wait a minute! The directive says 'a condition certified to be terminal by two physicians.' I want a second opinion." She asked the Mountain Manor staff to call another doctor. They said they only had one other doctor on call, that he was old and reluctant to come in, and that they would probably get in trouble with him for asking. My mother would not be dissuaded. The doctor was called. To the staff's surprise he said he would come immediately. The facility requested we call a lawyer because the directive was outdated. We contacted my parent's lawyer in San Francisco. He said whenever a person becomes incompetent, the directive has to be honored.

The old doctor came in. He examined my dad. He removed his stethoscope from his ears and reached for the paperwork, "I'll take this outside the room and read it over before signing it." Somehow, I think my dad understood because I saw a pleading look in his eyes as if he wanted to say, "Please, please, I don't want to live like this. Let me go." That settled it. As far as I was concerned, I would let him die with no further intervention. How could I possibly allow him to suffer?

In a few minutes, the administrator came back in the room, and to my amazement, told us the old doctor said: "I refuse to sign this man's life away. He may have a blood clot in his lungs or an entirely fixable condition."

Once more we shifted gears completely and called the ambulance to take him to the hospital. As I followed the ambulance I thought of the verse, "Neither know we what to do, but our eyes are on you," (II Chronicles 20:12).

*   *   *

When Dad arrived in the emergency room, the nurses were unable to get a blood pressure. His eyes were sunken. His pulse was rapid at 110, and he had a temperature of 101. His white count was 29,000. When his other lab work came back, the nurse told the doctor she'd never seen labs that bad in a living human being. When I faxed a copy of Dad's "panic-value" lab work to our family doctor, he said he couldn't believe he was still alive. I overheard the emergency room nurse say to the next shift, "Everyone is stable, but keep an eye on this guy."

Years ago, I was making home nursing visits to one of my best friends who was dying of cancer. Her sister-in-law, also an RN, told me, "You know you can do something about it. Just turn up her morphine, and ease her out until she quits breathing." I refused, because I believed that only God was the giver and taker of life. Now I faced another test of my faith. I used to think that nothing was more black and white than death, but now there were gray areas and blurred morals.

The technology of today puts physicians and nurses in a place we were never meant to be. No one should decide how valuable a life is except the one who created it. Psalms 104:29 says that God takes their breath away and they die. I believed that, that was his place, not mine. When I was discussing this with someone at the hospital, she said she was not sure she agreed with me. People may disagree, but when you have power of attorney for someone's life, it is an awesome responsibility. In the case of my friend and now my father, I wanted to leave it in God's hands—God who sees the whole picture—not in the hands of a human who can see only a part. I had to live with myself and my convictions.

On September twenty-fifth, the day after Dad's admission, the doctor told us not to get our hopes too high because Dad's kidneys were not functioning normally. My only hope was in the one who would do what was best. To make an eighty-eight year old man's kidneys start to function again would be nothing to God. That same day Dad tried to look around. The next day I told my mother we knew he wouldn't want to live like this, but we gave him a chance to die and he wouldn't die. Ecclesiastes says that there is a time to die, but I don't think my dad knew that, so he just kept on breathing. He was fighting for breath at three times faster than normal respiration.

When my mother and I arrived at the hospital the next day, the patient co-coordinator met us. "We've been waiting for you. We need to meet with you in our office." As we entered the office, we noticed the door to my dad's room was closed, and we prepared ourselves for the news that he had not made it through the night. Instead, the doctor told us Dad's kidneys had quit functioning and that he could not live without dialysis. Mother and I agreed. No dialysis, no ventilators, no feeding tubes, and no artificial means of support.

Then we went to his bedside to await the inevitable. Instead, to our amazement, as my mother patted him on the arm and turned to me, he lifted his arm and reached out to her. When we grabbed his hand, he squeezed ours. We asked him to open his eyes, and after we repeated it loudly over and over again, he opened them. He tried to look around. He was hanging onto life.

The hospital provided Mother a room free of charge, but I was driving back and forth from home to Medford, trying to keep up at work because I'd missed so much. I kept my car packed with clothes. In fact, I had more clothes in my car than I had at home.

Two days later, his kidneys started functioning again. One nurse said, "He's had 2400 cc's in and 2200 cc's out, that's better than me." A male nurse tried to swab out his mouth, and my dad shook his fists at him and tried to hit him. The following day, his respirations were finally below sixty a minute. His white count was up though, a sign of his body's attempt to fight infection. His labs improved, but his level of consciousness had not. When I asked the doctor why, he said he would back off the morphine and see if it made a difference. The doctor ordered further tests to see why the antibiotics weren't clearing the infection. We didn't know the source of the infection and nothing explained his continual decline and increasing pain.

Finally, the tests revealed an enlarged gall bladder. An abscess. They punctured it under CT (computed tomography, a type of radiography that shows a three dimensional image of a body structure) and attempted to drain the abscess since there was no way he could withstand surgery. My dad hung on.

We had no answers. The doctors had no answers. The only thing that kept me going was knowing that God did have answers. I called a friend and told her it would be devastating to think that my dad might live in this state, and that I was praying for God to either take his life or restore him. I told her I also had prayed that he would not die on my mother's birthday, about a week away on October fifth. She interrupted me, "Edna, you can't tell God what to do."

The hardest part was continually shifting gears. One day we would adjust to his inevitable dying. The next day the labs showed improvement, and the doctor would say that he had turned a corner. We would get our hopes up. Maybe he would pull through. And then our hopes were dashed when he had another set back. As his condition declined, we would prepare ourselves and call the family because we knew he couldn't possibly make it. Then we would go back to his room, and he would be resting comfortably. His potassium dropped from 6.6, a panic level that can cause cardiac arrhythmias and death, back to the normal range. One day he even had the Cheyne-Stokes breathing pattern, the final breathing pattern before death, but the next day he was breathing normally. The next time I visited, his eyes were open but not focusing or following. Their color had changed from dark brown to gray.

Waiting, waiting, waiting, and as we did we overheard the minor things that patients ring their bells for: "I have a little gas on my stomach." "My gown has a hole in it; could you bring me a new one?" "Aren't you going to come get my tray?" And all that time, my dad fought for his life. The next day my mother said, "He hasn't got enough left to walk out of this hospital, and maybe it's better."

On October second, the doctor suggested comfort measures only. His respirations were back to sixty a minute. His X-rays showed pneumonia, and he was moved to a hospice room. I prayed again that he would not die on my mother's birthday, which was in three days. When we went out for breakfast, the cheerful waitress breezed by with her pot of coffee, "Hi, how's your day going?" If I had said that my dad was hanging between life and death, she wouldn't have heard as she rushed off without waiting for an answer to pour coffee to the next customer. When I went back to the hospital, I could tell he was hydrated, which meant he could live for a few more days.

As soon as the hospital elevator opened when I arrived on October third, I could hear my dad's respirations clear down the hall. Shortly after I got to his room, the nurse came in and asked how I was doing. "I know there's an anger stage to death, and I'm there." Dad's loud, raspy, labored breathing was more than I could stand. I couldn't stay in the room any longer and watch him suffer. I ran to my car and wrote this prayer in my journal:

"Okay, God, hasn't my dad experienced enough? I am convinced he cannot live, but why won't you take his breath away? I look in the Bible for answers, and I see Job 3:21, "Which longs for death and it comes not." I have power of attorney for health care to tell them to keep increasing the morphine until his respirations stop, but I'm not God, and I don't pretend to play God. I no longer want to pray that he gets better or else you take his life. I am asking you for the first time that he dies today, that he not linger on. To hear his labored, rapid breathing way down the hall the minute the elevator opened, and then when I got to the room, to hear my mother talk about the funeral and burial plot, I could just scream. I thought you were a God of mercy. Where is your mercy, God? I thought you were a God of justice. Where is your justice, God? He is fighting so much to live, and his body won't give in. The doctor took away the IV's yesterday (the doctor's decision and my mother's). I am convinced now that he will not make it, but why won't you let him die as soon as possible? Please take away the struggle. You are the giver and taker of life. Please take his life away now. It has been eight days since we wanted to give him every possible chance to live. Why did you direct that doctor to say, "I'm not going to sign this man's life away," when we didn't want to prolong it and neither did my dad? Already his eyes are gray instead of brown, open, but not seeing. God, you made the body systems to function; you can make them shut down. He is struggling to breathe at sixty breaths a minute, and he won't give up. I am asking you to cause his respiratory system to quit breathing, his heart to stop beating, and his urinary system to shut down. No human would want to let him continue to live in this condition. 'Shall mortal man be more just than God?' (Job 4:17). God show your compassion, justice, and mercy and take his life today. We have done all we can, humanly, medically, and as a family. Now I ask that you arise and act and let him die today and not linger on. Because of his hearing loss he can't hear us when we tell him to quit fighting and let go. Because of his Alzheimer's, he can't understand. His heart is strong, and I can't make it stop beating. Please God, deal with his spirit, so he will not keep fighting to live. You can tell him on the inside what we can't tell him on the outside. Lord, your word says in Psalms 104:29, that 'you take away their breath and they die.' I am asking you to take my dad's breath away. I am asking you to take him home now and give him peace."

As soon as I finished writing my prayer, I returned to my dad's room. I noticed it was quiet when I walked down the hall. I entered the room and asked my mother when the change had happened. She said the change had occurred within the last five minutes. I counted his respirations at forty a minute instead of sixty. As I stood by his bed, my mother and I watched as his urine output gradually ceased. His respirations decreased to twenty and then to twelve and then to four and gradually stopped altogether. His heart stopped beating within ten minutes after my prayer in the car. My father died in peace.

Epilogue

Life can only be understood in reverse.

—Unknown

As we were leaving the hospital, so was a new mother holding her bundled baby as a nurse pushed her wheelchair though the double doors. A blue balloon announcing "It's a boy" was tied to the chair. The father was holding the car door open, eager to help his family. As I watched them I thought, one departed this life and another entered at almost the same time. "One generation passes away and another comes," (Ecclesiastes 1:4). It was the baby's time to enter the world and my dad's time to leave.

On the three-hour trip home, we passed a store front with a sign posted on the door, "Moved to a new location." I saw that sign and realized my dad had also moved to a new location, and the real Ray was now free of the Alzheimer's that had a chokehold on his mind. He was free of the body that shut down. He was free of the mind that tricked him. He was untouchable now.

The body dies but not the person. The mind dies but not the spirit. The real person, who we are on the inside, still lives. As John Henry Adams said before he died, "The thatched roof is almost off, the windows are cloudy, and I can barely see out, but John Henry is fine."

I don't believe that death was the end of my dad. As D.L. Moody said, "Someday you will read in the paper that I am dead. Don't you believe a word of it; I am more alive than I have ever been." As I look back on my father's life, I think it would not be fair to him if there weren't more to look forward to than life on earth. Edgar A. Guest said, "How purposeless the strife would be if there were nothing more, if there were not a plan to serve, an end to struggle for. There must be something after death; behind the toil of man . . . there must exist a God divine, who's working out a plan."

We were a little shocked to read what one of my mother's friends wrote in a sympathy card: "I am both saddened and relieved to hear of Ray's death." But we understood and had to admit she was right. Alzheimer's helped me let go when otherwise I never would have. I went from knowing that I could never bear to lose my dad to feeling a peace that he was gone and not suffering any longer. When mourners at the funeral said, "I'm sorry about your dad," I answered, "I miss him, but I could never wish him back." How could I wish him back to go through all he did with Alzheimer's and finally the agonizing last weeks of his life?

In the weeks that followed the funeral, my children and their spouses looked through the frames of Dad's arrowheads to select one as a keepsake from their Grandpa Ray. Scott chose a small rectangular one and said, "I remember when I was a boy hearing Grandpa Ray say, 'Someday, Scott, this frame will be hanging in your house.' Now I can pass it on to Hayden and Luke, along with Grandpa's work ethic, honesty, and advice about life."

Shelley, always the practical one said, "It's so sad to see Grandpa go, but because he was eighty-eight, the end was inevitable. If he had lived longer he would have continued to suffer because the Alzheimer's would have taken more of him." Then she shared a journal entry with us: "It doesn't seem possible that I find myself in this day in this year, where did all the time go between then and now? My last memory of Grandpa Ray is vivid. We teased each other across the table at Burger King in Redding. There was a familiar twinkle in his eyes. Even though I am sure that Alzheimer's wouldn't allow him to remember my name, I could tell somehow he knew me. We shared an occasional giggle. As far as he was concerned, he'd just gotten out of prison at a rest home, and he was happy as a lark. When he climbed into Mom and Dad's car, I gave him a huge hug and a kiss on the cheek. I giggled and teased him one last time, blew him a kiss, and that was it. I never saw him again. He lived for nine more months, and I never made the seven-hour journey to see him. All because I guarded that last memory of him quite dearly, but it was with a cost."

My mother could no longer sleep in the bed they had shared as a couple. She moved into their guest room. She kept busy with her social calendar, meetings, friends, and church potlucks. Her calendar was full, but nothing quite filled the void Dad left in her life. She was hungry for the companionship she once had. After my dad died, my son-in-law Tony said that Mother could "eat him under the table" at holiday dinners. She would help herself to another serving long after he finished eating, because she was hungry, not for food, but for the conversation and sense of belonging.

We had to move my dad a total of eight times in four years over a radius of 350 miles. But during that time, God never once failed to supply our needs and answer our prayers. He always directed us. He always provided a place for my dad. God made a way through, no matter how grim the situation was. I believe that there is a season and a purpose for everything. Even for the things I don't understand. In the end, it was Alzheimer's that was defeated. It had to let go of his mind when God released his spirit. "I have fought the good fight, I have finished my course, I have kept the faith," (II Timothy 4:7).

Dad was taken to a far better place where there is no sickness or disease. I know this was what he wanted. I believe he is in a place now where he hears without hearing aids, where his mind and emotions are intact, where he gardens without weeds, and where he enjoys the things he loves to do. I believe he is restored to wholeness. As Aunt Lillian wrote in her sympathy card, "He has just begun to live!"

I wish it had been easy for me to accept my dad's death. Eight months later, just before Father's Day, I realized his death hadn't really hit me yet. My husband has always been the one to pick out cards for any occasion. He came home with a small plastic bag. I peeked inside to see what he had selected. I was momentarily angry because he had chosen only one Father's Day card. Then I remembered I no longer had a father. I missed him terribly.

I used to find him in his hobby room chipping arrowheads or in his garden picking tomatoes or coming around the house with an armful of wood. After he was diagnosed, I missed the moments of clarity. I missed that rare spark of recognition in his eyes. I missed his presence no matter how bad he was physically or mentally. When he was no longer in his own home, I could always find him in a facility, good or bad. When he was no longer in California, I could find him in Oregon. But I always found him somewhere. Now he was just so gone. Right after his death, I couldn't cry or spend one minute wishing him back for his sake. Alzheimer's hold on him was finally broken. Now I could cry for me.

There is a memory forever etched in my mind. It was 1994. The kids were home from college. My parent's vitality was beginning to fade. Mother was frail and Dad was stooped and starting to slip a little mentally. Scott and Shelley had invited a couple of friends home from college to go to the fair with them. My mother invited all of us over for dinner. Mother cooked the traditional dinner of roast, vegetables, mashed potatoes and gravy. She knew from Scott and Shelley's letters that they had been trying to survive on their own cooking and what fast food they could grab between classes.

After we filed through the kitchen and filled our plates with the delicious home-cooked food, my parents sat in their usual places, one at each end of the dining room table. We sat on each side. We lingered talking and laughing until the meal was over, and the kids and Lennie left to go to the destruction derby. My mother cleared the table. I washed the dishes, and my dad dried. After we put the dishes away, it was time for me to go. My parents walked me across the street to my car in the early evening light. After I told them thank you, we said goodbye, and I headed toward home.

As I drove away, I looked back and waved. The image of my parents in the rear-view mirror remains with me after all these years. The sun was just setting as they walked back across the street. Their shadows lengthened and crossed the double line. I could see their silhouettes as my car picked up speed, and my parents became shadows against the sunset. They grew smaller as the car made greater distance between them and me. As I rounded the corner, they seemed to be mere specks, with barely lingering shadows, before they vanished from my sight.

That treasured image is a reflection of life: We go on, and our parents recede into the distance . . . into memories. A new generation is born and grows to maturity taking in everything around them, soaking up life. They develop and mature while the older generation gradually disappears in the distance.

Advice and Guidelines
for Caregivers

The Golden Rule Revisited

By Dr. Edwin Leap

They lie there, breathing heavy gasps, contracted into a fetal position. Ironic, that they should live eighty or ninety years, then return to the posture of their childhood. But they do. Sometimes their voices are mumbles and whispers like those of infants and toddlers. I have seen them, unaware of anything for decades, crying out for parents long since passed away.

I do not know what I see when I stand by the bedside of the infirm aged. Though their bodies are skin-covered sticks and their minds an inescapable labyrinth, I see something surprising. I see beautiful and horrible, hopeful and hopeless. What I see is my children, long after I leave them, as they end their days.

This vision comes to me sometimes when I stand by the bedside in my emergency department, and look over the ancient form that lies before me, barely aware of anything. Usually the feeling comes in those times when I am weary and frustrated from making too many decisions too fast in the middle of the night. Into the midst of this comes a patient from a local nursing home, sent for reasons I can seldom discern.

I walk into the room, and I roll my cynical eyes at the nurse. She hands me the minimal data sent with the patient, and I begin my detective work. And just when I am most annoyed, just when I want to do nothing and send them back, I look at them. And then I touch them. And then, as I imagine my sons, tears well up, and I see the error of my thoughts. For one day, it may be my sons.

One day, my little boys, still young enough to kiss me and think me heroic, may lie before another cynical doctor, in the middle of the night of their dementia, and need care. More than medicine, they need compassion. They need someone to have the insight to look at them and say: Here was once a child, cherished and loved, who played games in the nursery with his mother and father. Here was a child who put teeth under pillows and loved bedtime stories, crayons, and stuffed animals. Here was a treasure of love to a man and woman long gone. How can I honor them? By treating their child with love and gentility. By seeing that their child has come full circle to infancy once more and will soon be born once more, into forever.

My career as an emergency physician has taught me something very important about dealing with the sick and injured, whether young or old. It has taught me that the Golden Rule can also be stated this way: Do unto others as you would have others do unto your children.

Medication Guidelines for Caregivers

If there were one thing I could do over again in caring for my dad, it would be to deal with Alzheimer's without prescription drugs. I would use behavioral and environmental management instead. The drugs robbed us of what time we had left with my dad. They took more of my dad away from us than Alzheimer's would have taken alone. With the drugs, he became not only more forgetful and confused but wild-eyed and delirious. Without the drugs, his behavior would have been more predictable. The prescribed drugs made it impossible for us and the medical professionals to tell the difference between Alzheimer's symptoms and the side effects and interactions of the drugs. Another big side effect of the medication was the cost. My mother was soon paying more per month for the medications than she was for my dad's care.

Dad was always able to tie his shoes—even with severe Alzheimer's—unless he was over-medicated. When he was over-medicated, he could only sign his name with an "X." When medications were discontinued, he could tie his shoes again, sign his name in cursive, and once even drew a duck for us. I think he reacted especially poorly to prescription drugs because, throughout his life, he'd never taken more than an aspirin. He believed in letting things run their course rather than medicating himself, so his system was particularly sensitive.

He completed the course of all the Alzheimer's drugs available at the time but without any improvement that could be directly attributed to the medications. Our local physician said that if the drugs were supposed to slow the rate of progression, there was no way to measure that because Alzheimer's patients progress at their own rate, and no one knows what that rate is.

At times when Dad became increasingly difficult to handle, more prescriptions—called chemical restraints—were added to control his anger. He was placed on Tegretol, and the side effect was speech impairment.

Next my mother was instructed to give him Haldol, and the side effect was incontinence. The Haldol dosage was reduced when he was unable to zip his pants. Then he was given Paxil and Diazepam, and the side effect of both was increased confusion. When his behavior became out of control, which it did periodically—probably due to the Alzheimer's—he became agitated and aggressive. For that he was given Zyprexia, an anti-psychotic with a side effect of increased agitation. Then he was given Buspar, which brought on dizziness, over-stimulation, nervousness, incoordination, nightmares, and confusion. Then Ativan, with the side effects of dizziness, drowsiness, hallucinations, weakness, and unsteadiness. And lastly, a doctor prescribed Restoril, which again caused lethargy, drowsiness, dizziness, and confusion. Not only was my father experiencing the side effects of the individual drugs but the interactions of being on multiple drugs at the same time.

When chemical restraints compounded his behavior, the solution was always the same: "Move him immediately." Because he was transferred to so many facilities, his medication orders followed him. Precautions went unheeded, such as the warnings in drug handbooks that "caution must be used when anti-psychotics are given to elderly patients because metabolism is slowed and adverse reactions can occur rapidly."

The answer to managing my dad's Alzheimer's was not in chemically restraining him but in analyzing and managing his behavior. Eventually we realized that. We found and treated the causes of acting out instead of just adding another drug. More time spent in prevention meant less time patching up. A prescription for agitation didn't solve the problem when the real solution was in identifying and preventing what caused the behavior in the first place.

We looked for the simplest cause first. Did he need to find a bathroom? Could he be thirsty? Could he have a urinary tract infection, a common cause of confusion in the elderly. We kept a log to track what preceded the negative behavior. Having a log made it easier to determine what occurred outside of the normal daily routine. We'd ask ourselves: What in the environment was contributing to his behavior? Was there excessive commotion? Excessive noise? Was he rushed? Were there extra people present?" Questions like that allowed us to see what triggered his negative behavior and to figure out how to avoid it in the future. We avoided many problems when we controlled the environment and removed Dad from situations where stimuli were coming at him faster than he could process.

My dad's acting out occurred in cycles. He would be fine for a few months and then have a catastrophic episode. Drugs compounded the situation and turned a short-term issue into a long-term problem until the drugs were out of his system. Even when the drugs were discontinued, it took a while before he would be himself again.

If you choose to go with drugs, I recommend the following:

- Purchase a drug reference book. Study the drugs that are prescribed to your loved one and learn the dosage and frequency.
- Establish yourself with one pharmacist and consult him regarding side effects and interactions. Don't try to save money by getting prescriptions from multiple pharmacies or doctors. Stay with one pharmacy and one physician overseeing care.
- Schedule appointments with a family doctor on a regular basis. Take the patient's medications to the appointment, so the doctor can evaluate the effectiveness of the medication and determine if refills are necessary. Sometimes elderly people think they are supposed to have a prescription refilled just because the bottle is empty.
- Don't allow the patient to be sedated to the point of becoming a fall risk. The more drugs a patient is on, the greater the risk of falling, which is a major cause of fractured bones in the elderly. If a patient starts falling, request that the amount of medication or frequency be reduced. Don't assume patients fall just because they are elderly.
- See that the patient is monitored closely for interactions and toxicity.
- Request that the number of prescriptions or dosage of the drugs be reduced, so they don't build up in the patient's system. Older people don't metabolize drugs as well as younger adults. Drug manuals suggest that providers reduce dosage in the elderly and debilitated.
- Follow up to see that orders for tapering-off doses have not been overlooked.
- Request drug holidays or medication rests when possible.
- Be aware that any drug with a side effect of decreasing the appetite can decrease the vital nutrition necessary for proper brain functioning.
- Be aware that the side effects listed for a medication may be the same as the symptoms the medication is supposed to address.
- Understand that prescription drugs are a trade off, not a cure. For example, a specific drug may help control excessive activity and aggression, but it may cause increased confusion and incontinence.
- Request that a drug be discontinued when the side effects outweigh the potential benefits.

Each time psychotropic meds were added to my dad's regular medications, in an attempt to control his disruptive behavior, the side effects increased. The pattern was always the same and included the following side effects:

- Increased weakness, wobbliness, and unsteadiness; couldn't walk without tripping
- Dizziness
- Decreased appetite, weight loss
- Slurred speech
- Nodding off
- Increased urinary incontinence, decreased control of bowels
- "Wild-eyed," pinpoint or dilated pupils
- Drooling, when taking high dosages
- Lowered social inhibitions
- Increased confusion
- Increased paranoia
- Increased agitation, combativeness, restlessness; more difficult to control

When the medications were decreased, we observed the following:

- Alertness increased; drowsiness decreased
- Falls stopped
- Body weight increased
- Ability to communicate improved
- Recognition increased
- Awareness of his surroundings increased
- Anger and irritability decreased
- Frustration with caregivers decreased
- Behavior problems decreased
- Regained bladder and bowel control
- Walked independently; wheelchair no longer needed

My mother's personal journal entries about the man she lived with for over fifty years probably say more about the improvements in my dad's behavior when he was off drugs than any clinical list ever could. She wrote: "He smiled and offered his hand to Lennie." And, "Ray opened the door for us; he was smiling, and there was recognition is his eyes."

I know it pleased and relieved her to receive reports from caregivers like, "He has the kindest eyes of anyone I have ever known," and "He is a pleasure to have around." But I think the most tender moments for her were when he called her by name and kissed her hello, "There's my sweetheart, Ruth."

Practical Advice for Caregivers

It's important that family members and caregivers have a practical understanding of simple things that work with Alzheimer's patients. Knowing how to respond to Alzheimer's patients makes all the difference in their behavior. If the patient is upset about something, distract him for a while, and give his short-term memory a chance to engage to forget what he was upset about. If he is angry, walk away instead of trying to correct or reason with him.

Learn what diffuses a situation and what escalates it. A friend said her husband often asked her if he had fed the dog. She said they hadn't had a dog in twenty years, but she learned that rather than try to convince him of that, it was easier to say, "Yes, you have."

If you feel something isn't working or is making the situation worse, change whatever tactic you are using, or ask the patient's physician to change medications. It may also mean exploring options for placement in a quieter facility or setting. Go with your gut feelings.

Here are some guidelines we've gathered from our own experience and experiences of others, valid of course for both men and women patients:

- Consider basic needs first. Patients can't seek out food and water on their own; encourage frequent sips to prevent fluid and electrolyte imbalance; offer finger foods.
- Instead of trying to change the patient, change the environment.
- Trying to reason with the patient only causes frustration.
- Don't expect the patient to be manageable in an environment perceived as threatening.
- Eliminate commotion and minimize distraction. If necessary, remove the patient from those kinds of situations.

- Be attentive to hearing aids and glasses. Hearing aids can act as earplugs if ears are full of hair and wax; smeared glasses can obstruct vision.
- If your patient is in a care facility, purchase easily identifiable personal items for the patient, and label hearing aids, false teeth, slippers, etc.
- Rather than risk losing the patient's wedding ring, considering substituting it before admission to a care facility.
- Let the facility know if the patient has a partial plate or dentures, so dental ware can be properly maintained and cleaned.
- To help assure better, more consistent patient care at a facility, vary the times of your visits to coincide with different work shifts. If the staff is aware that family and friends make frequent visits and at varying times during the day, they are apt to be more attentive to the patient's needs.
- If the patient resists what you are doing, walk away and give him time to forget, then try again in a few minutes. Use diversion to redirect the patient from something he is upset about.
- Leave the room if the patient is upset.
- If the patient wanders, walk with him until he tires.
- Understand that you can never win an argument with an Alzheimer's patient.
- Speak in simple short sentences, and give the patient time to process what you are saying.
- Give clear, short commands one at a time. Don't give multiple requests at once.
- Write notes and refer the patient to the notes when he asks repeated questions.
- Remember that the patient picks up on your mood first and your words second.
- Patients understand more than they can verbalize; don't talk about them in front of them. They know when they are not wanted or are being talked about negatively.
- Don't startle the patient by approaching from behind or grabbing and attempting to move him quickly.
- Don't expect him to do things he can no longer do.
- Even small difficulties can cause major frustration for the patient.
- Simplify daily chores and routines.
- To help ensure success rather than frustration, give patients responsibilities and activities consistent with their past interests and abilities.
- Enter their world; don't expect them to enter yours.

- Don't over-stimulate the patient.
- Make changes slowly; never rush.
- Keep a log of reactions and behaviors and what triggers disruptive or agitated behavior.
- Try to keep your patient mentally and physically active.
- Eliminate or minimize choices. For example, don't make patients choose where, when, and what to eat. Maintain a consistent routine for personal hygiene, meals, etc.
- Encourage humor, they will laugh with you.
- Anticipate hazards; remove harmful liquids that could be mistaken for lotion or something to drink. If the patient lives with you, modify your home environment to reduce hazards.
- Avoid noise overload and noises the patient cannot interpret.
- If the patient is increasingly confused or agitated, ask that the patient be tested for a urinary tract infection. Confusion and agitation can be symptoms of a UTI.
- Check for sources of pain and discomfort. Have one primary-care physician for your patient.
- Alzheimer's patients have basic human needs for touch, recognition, and a feeling of belonging.
- Don't rob patients of their dignity.

Caregiver Care

My Aunt Helen, who was very close to my mother, told me one day while my dad was still alive, "I think that dealing with Ray's Alzheimer's is harder on Ruth than his death would be." That assessment summarizes the plight of many Alzheimer's caregivers. The weight of responsibility for another's life and well being is huge in the best of times, and that responsibility is compounded by the worry and frustration of knowing the Alzheimer's patient is only going to get worse. With family members, in addition to the twenty-four-hour care of the patient, all decision-making that was formerly shared now rests squarely on the caregivers. The burdens and challenges can be overwhelming. They can consume all of your energy and strength.

Plan ahead. While you and your spouse are still mentally competent, consult with an attorney to complete such documents as an advance directive, a durable power of attorney, or a trust to manage property and personal affairs when the need arises.

When you are a caregiver, it's vital that you take care of yourself mentally and physically. It's all too easy to get so wrapped up in the worry and stress of caregiving that you forget to take care of yourself, and ultimately you and the patient both suffer.

- Ask your doctor about Alzheimer's caregiver resources in your area, and access the many resources available on the Internet. Internet sites offer not only information but also support and understanding by being a platform to communicate with people coping with similar circumstances.
- Be attentive to financial practicalities associated with caring for a spouse or family member with Alzheimer's. Read the fine print of the

patient's long-term care policy. Be sure that the placement options being considered match the policy's care-facility criteria.

- If you are caregiving at home, schedule regular respite days for yourself by having a competent friend, relative, or a daycare provider come in or by taking your patient to a facility for a day or overnight stay.
- As much as possible, find a way to keep doing at least some of the activities and hobbies you enjoy. Develop and nurture an interest in a hobby not related to caregiving.
- Maintain and honor your friendships as much as possible. Stay in touch with people you care about. Don't isolate yourself.
- Try to "roll with the flow" of the patient's reality, and adjust your actions and reactions to fit the situations. Be prepared for the unexpected, both positive and negative. Don't take insults personally.
- Save yourself the frustration of trying to correct the patient. Instead enter the patient's world.
- Understand that you may go through the grieving process—denial, anger, bargaining, depression, and finally acceptance of the loss—while your loved one is still alive.

CPSIA information can be obtained at www.ICGtesting.com
Printed in the USA
LVOW040930110412

277115LV00001B/48/P